Your LIFE follows Your WORDS

RELEASING THE PRAYER OF FAITH

DARLENE BISHOP

Foreword by ROD PARSLEY

LEGACY
PUBLISHERS INTERNATIONAL

Unless otherwise indicated, all Scripture quotations are from the King James Version of the Bible. References marked "Moffatt" are from *A New Translation of the Bible* by James Moffatt, copyright © 1954, 1964 by James Moffatt. References marked "Rieu" are from *The Acts of the Apostles* translated by C.H. Rieu, copyright © 1957 by C.H. Rieu. Definitions marked *Strong's* are from *Strong's Exhaustive Concordance of the Bible,* Dugan Publishers, Inc., Gordonsville, Tennessee.

DISCLAIMER: Darlene Bishop is not a physician and does not intend, by anything that she says in this book, to be dispensing medical advice to the reader. She encourages each individual to seek God for their own avenue of healing. You should consult a physician before changing your medication or discontinuing any prescribed treatment. Any health advice adopted from this book by the reader is done at his or her own risk. If additional health advice is needed, seek the advice of your health professional. Neither the author of this book nor Legacy Publishers International has any liability whatsoever in regard to loss, damage, or injury suffered directly or indirectly as a result of the information contained in this book.

YOUR LIFE FOLLOWS YOUR WORDS: Releasing the Prayer of Faith
ISBN 1-880809-82-6

Printed in the United States of America
Copyright © 2004 by Darlene Bishop

Legacy Publishers International
1301 South Clinton Street
Denver, CO 80247
Phone: 303-283-7480 FAX: 303-283-7536

Library of Congress Cataloging-in-Publication Data Pending

DEDICATION

This book is dedicated to our congregation at Solid Rock Church, my babies who are continually praying for me and encouraging me. To you I say, B- E- L- I- E- V- E.

ACKNOWLEDGMENTS

First and foremost, I would like to give thanks to **my Lord and Savior, Jesus Christ**, for entrusting to me this revelation to impart to His Body.

To **my husband Lawrence** for all the sacrifices he has made. I know it's been hard, Baby, but you finally did learn how to use the microwave. Thank you for continually covering me in prayer.

To **my daughters—Jana, Renee, and Julie—and my only begotten son, Lawrence II**, for their willingness to allow me to fulfill my God-given purpose in life.

To **my brother Wayne**, who has fought the good fight of faith. It was *your* test that started me on this journey.

To **my assistant Shawna Halsey**, without whose help the Lord knew I could not do all that He has called me to do.

To **Arlene Parker**, the dearest friend God has ever given. Thank you for being willing to give of yourself.

To **the staff of Legacy Publishers International**, for believing in me and seeing this project through to fruition.

CONTENTS

FOREWORD BY ROD PARSLEY

When I hear someone preaching on the subject of prayer or faith, I look at their life as much as I listen to their words. I want to know if they have been through some things on the way to their revelation. Have they been tested in the fires of adversity and prayed their way through? Or are they just repeating truths someone else has reached into the realm of human experience to receive?

Darlene Bishop is not only one of the most powerful prayer warriors I know; she is also someone who has passed through the fire and come out on the other side purified and possessed with a desire to see all the members of the Body of Christ rise up and receive what belongs to them. Here, in her strong and straightforward manner, she gives us a greater understanding of the prayer of faith and the significance of the spoken word.

If you are looking for sound instruction and good news just the way Jesus preached it—plainly and powerfully—you will appreciate this book. And the principles it puts forth will forever change the way you approach prayer.

Pastor Rod Parsley
World Harvest Church
Columbus, Ohio

INTRODUCTION

Late in 2002 I received a phone call with some very bad news, news that took me off guard and hit me like a ton of bricks. My baby brother Wayne had been diagnosed with inoperable throat cancer, and his doctors had given him only six to eighteen months to live. This totally unexpected announcement seemed to knock the breath out of me and leave me gasping for air, just as I had experienced as a kid when one of my brothers would deliver a blow to my stomach.

I was the only girl at home at the time, my older sisters having already married, and so I had to learn to defend myself against four brothers. We fought, and sometimes when we did, one of them would hit me so hard in the stomach that all of the breath would leave me. For a time I would lie on the ground helplessly gasping for air, wondering if I would live or die. Those moments seemed interminable. I felt exactly the same emotions now. I was devastated and walked around the house in a daze.

Only fifty-two years old, Wayne was a successful songwriter who had been working in Nashville. He had written for Tim McGraw, the Backstreet Boys, and other well known country singers. Now he was in a car headed my way. Within hours he would be arriving.

I was his sister, but I was more. I was a pastor, a woman of God, and he expected me to have some answers for him when he got there. "I need you now, Sis," he said before hanging up, "as never before." What would I tell Wayne when he arrived? What could I tell him?

Yes, we believed in healing, and we had been preaching healing and praying for sick people for more than twenty years. I had even received a miraculous healing myself from cancer. But I had also known many people who had been prayed for and had *not* been healed. I had already lost one sister to cancer, and another sister

9

was suffering from cancer at the time. What was wrong with our Christian concept of healing? It seemed so simple and easy to understand and teach, and yet it often didn't work for us. Why?

As a child, when my breath finally did come back to me, I would be so angry that my brothers knew they had better run the other way. Not one of them could get in another hit ... until the next time we fought. And now, as my breath began to come normally to me again, I got very angry. How dare the devil try to afflict my brother! He had no right to do that! I reared back in my anger and let the enemy know that he had not defeated me. Far from it. If Wayne had cancer, then this was an opportunity to watch God work, and I got serious in prayer and in searching God's Word for answers to make it happen.

What I found in the coming hours came as a revelation, and it transformed my life and ministry. Wayne would live. I would see to that. God had promised him healing, and I would see to it that he received it.

As the New Year dawned, I had a fresh new teaching, and that teaching brought great revival to the church my husband Lawrence and I pastor (Solid Rock Church in Monroe, Ohio). Not only were our people stirred and challenged, but many new faces were added to our membership. This message also blessed other groups as I preached it in conferences and churches around the country.

Now, through the pages of this book, I am able to share this message for the first time in print to a wider audience. I am convinced that it will revolutionize *your* way of thinking as well. Hold on to your seat as together we uncover truths that most of us have never encountered before, truths that will enable us all to minister more effectively to the many sick around us, to pray, with power and authority, the prayer of faith.

Darlene Bishop
Solid Rock Church
Monroe, Ohio

Is any among you afflicted? let him pray. Is any merry? let him sing psalms. Is any sick among you? let him call for the elders of the church; and let them pray over him, anointing him with oil in the name of the Lord: and THE PRAYER OF FAITH SHALL SAVE THE SICK, and the Lord shall raise him up; and if he have committed sins, they shall be forgiven him. Confess your faults one to another, and pray one for another, that ye may be healed. THE EFFECTUAL FERVENT PRAYER OF A RIGHTEOUS MAN AVAILETH MUCH. Elias was a man subject to like passions as we are, and he prayed earnestly that it might not rain: and it rained not on the earth by the space of three years and six months. And he prayed again, and the heaven gave rain, and the earth brought forth her fruit.

James 5:13-18

Chapter 1

A New Year and a New Decree

Thou shalt also decree a thing, and IT SHALL BE ESTAB-
LISHED UNTO THEE: and the light shall shine upon thy ways.

Job 22:28

The news of Wayne's sickness and the fact that he was that very moment on his way to my house to be prayed for (and he was expecting answers) drove me to prayer and to study what the Word of God had to say about healing as never before. My mind kept going back to the promise of James: *"The prayer of faith shall save the sick"* (James 5:15). That was the answer, and it seemed to be so cut and dried. But what were we missing? Why wasn't this promise working more for Christians everywhere? We were praying, but people were dying anyway? Clearly something was wrong. What was it?

Was the problem in our attitudes? Was it in the words we were praying? The more I looked at James 5:15, the more I became convinced that there was something the Lord was trying to show me about it:

And the prayer of faith shall save the sick, and the Lord shall
raise him up. James 5:15

The word *save* seemed to jump off of the page at me:

Save ..., save .... , save ... . The prayer of faith shall SAVE the sick.

13

What did it mean to *save* the sick? I thought I had known, but apparently I hadn't.

Gradually I became convinced that the words I was reading had to mean much more than my surface understanding of them, and I was prompted to look up the words *save* and *saved* in my *Strong's Concordance*.

The Benefits Package That Comes with Salvation

I found this word again in Romans 10, where Paul wrote to the believers in that ancient capitol of the world:

> *If thou shalt confess with thy mouth the Lord Jesus, and shalt believe in thine heart that God hath raised him from the dead, thou shalt be SAVED. For with the heart man believeth unto righteousness; and with the mouth confession is made unto SALVATION. For the scripture saith, Whosoever believeth on him shall not be ashamed. For there is no difference between the Jew and the Greek: for the same Lord over all is rich unto all that call upon him. For whosoever shall call upon the name of the Lord shall be SAVED.* **Romans 10:9-13**

Was this a different *saved* than the *saved* found in James 5:15? The concordance showed that it was *not* different. James spoke of the prayer of faith saving the sick, and Romans spoke of salvation from sin. Apparently, the word *saved* in the Scriptures meant far more than just escaping from Satan, hell, and judgment, as we had been accustomed to believe. There were many other benefits to salvation.

As I read the meaning of the word *saved* given by *Strong's*, I realized that this was the case. According to the concordance, *saved* also meant being delivered, being healed, being protected, being preserved, and being made whole. With that discovery, my soul filled with rejoicing, and I did as David had done in Psalm 103; I began to bless the Lord:

Bless the LORD, O my soul: and all that is within me, bless his holy name.
Bless the LORD, O my soul, and forget not all his benefits:
Psalm 103:1-2

There it was again: *"ALL HIS BENEFITS."* Believing in the Lord brings many benefits, not just forgiveness from sins. David was happy because the Lord was forgiving of all of his iniquities, but he was also rejoicing because the Lord, in the same way, was the Healer of all his diseases. And there was much more:

> *Believing in the Lord brings many benefits, not just forgiveness from sins.*

Who forgiveth all thine iniquities; who healeth all thy diseases;
Who redeemeth thy life from destruction; who crowneth thee with lovingkindness and tender mercies;
Who satisfieth thy mouth with good things; so that thy youth is renewed like the eagle's. Psalm 103:3-5

There it was spelled out for me in detail. All of these wonderful blessings were the result of our salvation. How awesome!

I looked at it one more time:

Who forgiveth all thine iniquities [salvation from sin]
who healeth all thy diseases [healing from sickness]

YOUR LIFE FOLLOWS YOUR WORDS

Who redeemeth thy life from destruction [deliverance and protection]
who crowneth thee with lovingkindness and tender mercies
Who satisfieth thy mouth with good things; so that thy youth is renewed like the eagle's [preservation and wholeness]

It was perfectly outlined. Salvation was not just forgiveness from sin and escape from judgment and hell; it was much more. It was a complete package of benefits that included healing.

In that moment I felt like Isaiah did in the Temple when confronted by the presence of God:

In the year that king Uzziah died I saw also the Lord sitting upon a throne, high and lifted up, and his train filled the temple.

Isaiah 6:1

Isaiah's response had been to feel his own unworthiness:

Then said I, Woe is me! for I am undone; because I am a man of unclean lips, and I dwell in the midst of a people of unclean lips: for mine eyes have seen the King, the Lord of hosts.

Isaiah 6:5

Suddenly I felt very foolish. We had been taught (and had ourselves taught) that when we received Christ, we received spiritual salvation alone—the forgiveness of sins and the promise of eternal life. Sometime in the future we could receive healing, deliverance, protection, preservation, and wholeness, but in distinctly separate and miraculous encounters with God. Now I realized that this was not the case. We receive all of these benefits at once when we are saved, in the very moment we initially give our hearts to Jesus and receive Him as our Lord and Savior. What a revelation this was to me in that moment!

For those of us who are saved, or have received Christ as Savior from sins, our needs are already met. The problem is that we have been taught wrong, that salvation is one work and healing is another. In truth, it is all part of the same package.

I had been just as guilty as others of teaching these wrong concepts, but now I saw that when Christ died on Calvary, His work was completed then and there. James spoke of the sick being *saved* (from sickness) through the prayer of faith, and Paul wrote to the Romans about the lost being *saved* (from the punishment for sin) through repentance and confession, but they were talking about the same blessing. Being "saved" includes physical healing, as well as forgiveness from sins. In theory then we cannot be healed without being saved from sin, and we cannot be saved from sin without being healed. They are part of the same salvation package.

This fact is very evident in Matthew's account of the man who was sick of the palsy:

> *And he entered into a ship and passed over, and came into his own city. And, behold, they brought to him a man sick of the palsy, lying on a bed: and Jesus seeing this faith said unto the sick of the palsy; Son, be of good cheer; thy sins be forgiven thee. And, behold, certain of the scribes said within themselves, This man blasphemeth. And Jesus knowing their thoughts said, Wherefore think ye evil in your hearts? For whether is easier, to say, Thy sins be forgiven thee; or to say, Arise, and walk? But that ye may know that the son of man hath power on earth to forgive sins, (then saith he to the sick of the palsy,) Arise, take up thy bed, and go unto thine house.*
>
> Matthew 9:1-6

Jesus asked the question: which was easier, to save from sins or to heal? This shows very clearly that the saving of the soul and the healing of the body were (and are) one and the same work.

When God brought the children of Israel out of Egyptian bondage, Moses told them:

> *If thou wilt diligently hearken to the voice of the Lord thy God, and wilt do that which is right in his sight, and wilt give ear to his commandments, and keep all his statutes, I will put NONE OF THESE DISEASES upon thee which I have brought upon the Egyptians: for I am the Lord that healeth thee.*
>
> Exodus 15:26

> *God's desire for us is that we prosper and be in health.*

Disease is from the enemy, and it is not God's will for His people to be sick. He does not want any of His children to be feeble. This was proven when the Hebrews were leaving Egypt, and the Scriptures declare that there was *"not one feeble person"* among them:

> *He brought them forth also with silver and gold: and there was not one feeble person among their tribes.* Psalm 105:37

Not Only Health, But Also Wealth

God not only delivered His people from bondage; He also healed them of their illnesses and blessed them with abundant material riches.

These people had been slaves for generations in Egypt, and they had essentially nothing to take with them when they left that place.

A New Year and a New Decree

But God had told them to borrow from their owners everything they needed, and, amazingly, their owners gave them everything they asked for. Moses recounted exactly what they had thus inherited from the Egyptians:

> *And the children of Israel did according to the word of Moses; and they borrowed of the Egyptians jewels of silver, and jewels of gold, and raiment: And the Lord gave them favour in the sight of the Egyptians, so that they lent unto them such things as they required. And they spoiled the Egyptians.*
>
> Exodus 12:35-36

The Exodus from Egypt is a type of our exodus from the life of sin. And once we have left the slavery of sin, God's desire for us is that we prosper and be in health, even as our soul prospers. He said so Himself:

> *Beloved, I wish above all things that thou mayest prosper and be in health, even as thy soul prospereth.*   3 John 2

Sadly, most of us are not walking in this prosperity and health that God has ordained for us, and, because of it, we are living far beneath our privileges. There is much more to our salvation that we have not yet appropriated.

Not only are we given prosperity and health; we are also given power and authority to *"cure"* others:

> *Then he called his twelve disciples together, and gave them power and authority over all devils, and to cure diseases. And he sent them to preach the kingdom of God, and to heal the sick.*   Luke 9:1-2

YOUR LIFE FOLLOWS YOUR WORDS

Jesus called His disciples and deputized them, much like a sheriff with his posse in the times of the wild West. Thus, He enabled His disciples to defeat Satan and to cure diseases. And now the entire New Testament Church has been given this authority by Christ.

Jesus gave us power and authority to preach the Kingdom of God *and* to heal the sick, and it is wrong to do one without the other. They are part of the same package. If healing is not for today, as many assert, then neither is salvation from sin for today. They go together. Our commission to proclaim both still stands.

In many of our churches, we err in our approach to those in need. We invite sinners to the altar to receive salvation from sin, and then we tell them to come back that night to get in the prayer line for healing. We should begin to teach people, "When you were saved from sin, you were also healed. Now, walk in it." And when a person who is not yet saved comes to Christ for healing, we must assure them that their healing is part of the salvation package. One act opens the door for the other. Salvation brings with it many other wonderful blessings.

This concept of a package deal should not be strange to us. When someone is hired these days by a reputable company, their position usually comes with a benefits package. Along with a designated hourly or weekly wage, the employee may receive paid sick days, paid personal days, paid holidays, paid dental and medical insurance, free parking, free use of the company exercise room, free lunch and/or any number of other perks. This means that the employee is not just earning an agreed-upon wage; he or she is actually earning much more—when all the benefits are factored in.

We are saved, and that includes being healed, delivered, protected, preserved, and made whole in the name of Jesus. Oh, thank God for that! This truth makes us free, and once we receive this truth, we have no more need.

Christ's Completed Work On Calvary

When Christ died for us on Calvary, He completed the work. He paid the price for our forgiveness from sin, so we are saved:

> *For whosoever shall call upon the name of the Lord shall be SAVED.* Romans 10:13

It's guaranteed because He finished the work on Calvary. Peter recognized this and more when he said:

> *Who his own self bare our sins in his own body on the tree, that we, being dead to sins, should live unto righteousness: by whose stripes ye were HEALED.* 1 Peter 2:24

So Jesus paid the price for our salvation (taking our sins upon Himself), but He also paid the price for our healing (taking the stripes upon His back). Peter concluded from this that we *"were healed."* It is done. Christ paid the necessary price on Calvary.

Isaiah agreed:

> *He* **was** *wounded for our transgressions,* **he** **was** *bruised for our iniquities: the chastisement of our peace* **was** *upon him; and with his stripes we are HEALED.* Isaiah 53:5

It is finished.

Jesus has already paid the price to deliver us. He completed it there on the cross:

YOUR LIFE FOLLOWS YOUR WORDS

> *The Lord knoweth how to DELIVER the godly out of temptations.*
> 2 Peter 2:9

Jesus already paid the price for our protection. The Word declares:

> *The angel of the LORD ENCAMPETH ROUND ABOUT THEM that fear him, and DELIVERETH them.*
> Psalm 34:7

Jesus already paid the price for our preservation:

> *The LORD shall PRESERVE thee from all evil: he shall PRESERVE thy soul.*
> Psalm 121:7

Jesus paid the price for our wholeness:

> *The young lions do lack, and suffer hunger: but they that seek the LORD shall not want any good thing.*
> Psalm 34:10

We now want for nothing because of our Lord's sacrifice. David understood this truth in his day, having a foreshadow of things to come:

> *The LORD is my shepherd; I shall not want.*
> Psalm 23:1

How is it possible that we should want for *"nothing"*? Because Jesus has already provided everything we will ever need. What a great truth!

We Are Devil-Proofed At Salvation

This package of benefits makes us, as believers in Christ, devil proof. We have many promises that show it to be true:

A New Year and a New Decree

We are MORE THAN CONQUERORS through him that loved us. Romans 8:37

ALL POWER is given unto me in heaven and in earth. Go ye therefore ... . Matthew 28:18-19

Then he called his twelve disciples together, and gave them power and authority over all devils, and to cure diseases. And he sent them to preach the kingdom of God, and to heal the sick. Luke 9:1-2

Behold, I give unto you POWER to tread on serpents and scorpions, and OVER ALL THE POWER OF THE ENEMY: and NOTHING shall BY ANY MEANS hurt you. Luke 10:19

Greater is he that is in you, than he that is in the world. 1 John 4:4

If we are devil-proofed when we are saved, how is it then that the enemy sometimes is able to ride roughshod over us? How has he gained access to our lives? How is he able to *"hurt"* us? The only place the enemy can find to get into our lives is the place we give him through our ignorance. This is the reason the early believers were instructed:

Neither GIVE PLACE to the devil. Ephesians 4:27

Satan has gained a *"place"* in many of our lives, but I trust that through what you can learn in this book, the door will be shut again to him, and that you can again walk in total victory, rejoicing in all the elements of your salvation.

The Birth of the Decree

I found these revelations to be so exciting that I was spurred to action. As we moved into the New Year, I had a new decree ready based on these teachings, and I introduced it to our church as "My Decree." In it, I listed the benefits of salvation as they had been revealed to me, and with each one a scriptural passage to back it up. On the bottom of the page, we gave the promise of Psalm 103:3-5 and showed how it applied to each of the areas of salvation.

> *If we are devil-proofed when we are saved, how is it then that the enemy sometimes is able to ride roughshod over us?*

We printed copies of this decree and handed them out to every member, recommending that our people pray it every day, starting off each new day right by declaring their standing in God, and then doing the same in the evening before they went to bed, ending the day on that high note.

The decree and the corresponding promises are recorded on the final page of this book just as we presented them to our people many months ago. I hope that you will make copies of it and use it in your own way. Based on this new and revolutionary revelation I had received from God's Word, it says this:

I am saved.
I am healed.
I am delivered.
I am protected.
I am preserved.
I am made whole ... in the name of Jesus.

A New Year and a New Decree

There was much more to learn, and as I learned it myself, I began a teaching in our church that lasted sixteen weeks. The audio tapes of that teaching are available to those who are interested. * But for all of those who are ready to discover more through reading this book, let us now take another step.

* www.solidrockchurch.org

Chapter 2

THE NECESSARY CONFESSION

IF THOU SHALT CONFESS WITH THY MOUTH the Lord Jesus, and shalt believe in thine heart that God hath raised him from the dead, THOU SHALT BE SAVED. For with the heart man believeth unto righteousness; and WITH THE MOUTH CONFESSION IS MADE UNTO SALVATION. For the scripture saith, Whosoever believeth on him shall not be ashamed. For there is no difference between the Jew and the Greek: for the same Lord over all is rich unto all that call upon him. For whosoever shall call upon the name of the Lord shall be saved. Romans 10:9-13

The prayer of faith is a prayer of confession, affirmation, or decree.

The second thing that stood out to me as I began my review of the scriptural promises on healing were the many ways confession was tied to healing. This was more noticeable to me than it might otherwise have been because I had been teaching a series of messages in our church on the power of the tongue. Now I was seeing this power in a new light.

A proper confession and the power of our words was nothing new to me. I had been impacted by it my whole life. My father had been very good at making a positive confession over me when I was still a small child of preschool age. He told me and others around me that I would one day be an anointed servant of God, a preacher of the Gospel. Therefore, when God called me to the ministry, it came as no surprise. I had never forgotten my father's words, and they kept me through the intervening years.

Everything in Life
Comes to Us By Confession

Everything we have in life must be confessed before it is possessed. We do not receive anything without first confessing it. It is clear from the Scriptures that we cannot be saved from sin without confessing it. Some may think they are saved and have kept their experience a total secret, but they're wrong. It is impossible to be saved from sin without declaring it. Salvation must be confessed in order to be validated.

Most of us have had the experience of receiving a new credit card in the mail. On the card there's a sticker that gives a toll-free telephone number to call or an Internet address to visit to validate the card. If the card is not validated, it cannot be used.

This is exactly the way God's favor operates in our lives. He requires that we validate our salvation before it will work. Our every desire must be expressed with our mouths before we can actually receive it.

This is what Job meant when he said: *"Thou shalt also decree a thing, and it shall be established unto thee: and the light shall shine upon thy ways"* (Job 22:28). What this tells us is that we have to make a decision, and once we have made the decision, God will make it good. We decree it, and God establishes it. We confess a desire, and God brings it to pass.

It was with this principal in mind that Solid Rock Church adopted its decree for the year 2003 (the one I have included on the final page of this book). The decree is based on the word *saved*, as found here in Romans 10:9-10 and our discovery that the word not only means that I am saved, upon belief and confession, from Satan, hell, and judgment, but that there are many other benefits identified with salvation. As I stated in the previous chapter, I encourage you to make this decree your own. Repeat it aloud each morning and each evening so that you can walk in health and wealth and have need of nothing.

Get into your spirit the truth that God can do nothing in your life except you decree it first. The Scriptures declare very forcefully:

> *Everything we have in life must be confessed before it is possessed.*

Ye have not BECAUSE YE ASK NOT. James 4:2

If ye shall ASK ANY THING in my name, I WILL DO IT. John 14:14

This is the Word of God, and if we believe it, we will put forth a positive confession each day of our lives. Declare forcefully, "I am saved, I am healed, I am delivered, I am protected, I am preserved, I am made whole in the name of Jesus," and then start living it out because it is yours.

Keep Your Decree Before You

Put your decree up somewhere where you will see it every day. You might want to place it on your bathroom mirror where you will see it while you're getting dressed every morning. Place it somewhere prominently in your car so that you will see it and meditate on it as you are driving to work or commuting to school. Put it up on your refrigerator with your other notices so that you will see it every time you open the door to get something to eat or drink. If you are overweight, include an extra declaration of weight loss on your decree. The simple reason that many people are suffering from diabetes, high blood pressure, and cancer is that they are much too overweight. If this is true with you, every time you go to the refrigerator to get something to munch on, look at your declaration and tell the devil No! He loves it when we are overweight, because he wants to kill us anyway he can. Inform him that he will not be taking you out so easily.

Some of you might want to place your decree over your kitchen sink so that you will see it while you are preparing meals and washing dishes. Others, those who spend a lot of time in an office, might want to put it somewhere prominently over, on, or around your desk. Whereever you choose, keep your decree before your eyes so that the enemy cannot make you forget who you are and what you have in Christ.

Examine the printed decree and read carefully the scriptural benefits listed with each part of it. Reading the corresponding scripture aloud reinforces that particular confession.

With the sacred scriptures to back up your confession, you are thoroughly equipped, and you can make your daily declaration. Boldly tell the enemy of your soul, "I am saved, healed, delivered, protected, preserved, and made whole in the name of Jesus, and I want for nothing because I am in Christ." With this, he will flee.

The Confession of Salvation from Sin vs. the Confession of Physical Healing

We have long accepted the fact that we must confess with our mouths in order to receive spiritual salvation, but now God had revealed to me that we must also apply this same principal for receiving the other benefits awarded us as part of our salvation. We must confess healing, we must confess deliverance, we must confess protection, we must confess preservation, and we must confess being made whole—if we are to receive these blessings from God's hands. If we will confess them, we will see the manifestation of them.

As I said at the outset, this revelation totally changed my life and ministry. Because I now thought so differently about salvation, I also preached it differently, and this brought a new fruitfulness to my ministry. Our church people noticed it, and many others did as well.

When you think about it, it's only logical. If you are saved, as we have commonly used the term in the past, do you think God would withhold from you the other benefits of the salvation package? Of course not. They are yours. All you have to do is declare it. Make your confession: "I have the whole package."

We have confessed lies long enough, having believed what the enemy has said. But when we get the truths of this decree into our spirits, by seeing it before our eyes and putting it into our hearts, everything about us will change. We will talk differently, and when our talk changes, then our walk will also change.

Jesus taught very strongly this power of positive confession. One example that we will use throughout the book is found in the Gospel of Mark. He said:

> *Have faith in God. For verily I say unto you, That whosoever shall SAY unto this mountain, Be thou removed, and be thou cast into the sea; and shall not doubt in his heart, but shall believe that those things which he SAITH shall come to pass; he shall have whatsoever he SAITH. Therefore I say unto you, What things soever ye desire, when ye pray, believe that ye receive them, and ye shall have them.* Mark 11:22-24

The meaning of this passage seems shocking to many people, but it is there in plain English for all to see. We are to pray our desires. This is a very important concept and one that we will be learning more about as we go along. Most people pray what they have, rather than what they desire, so they keep what they have and never make any progress toward what they desire.

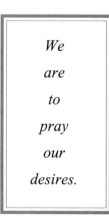

We are to pray our desires.

Aside from this, Jesus was showing us that we must be careful about what we say even in our prayers because whatever we say—good or bad—we will have. You can turn things around by starting to talk differently, and you can do it by using the promises of the Word of God. Every word in the Bible is a loaded bullet. It's like dynamite. Learn to confess it and receive it.

Two Kinds of Confession

There are two kinds of confession. This is important because I would not want anyone to think that I am teaching something that is not good Christian doctrine. One kind of confession is based upon the mind. It is a philosophy born out of knowledge. This is the doctrine Christian Science promotes. It encourages a person to employ the psychological defense of denial by saying, "This illness is not in my body." This is a mind-over-matter philosophy.

True Christians have the Word of God in their hearts and minds, and this marks the second type of confession. This confession is based upon the truth of the Word of God. In the face of a negative prognosis from your doctor, you can say, "Although the doctor reports that I have such and such a disease, Jesus said that this disease was already laid upon Him at Calvary. And, since He took it, I don't have to take it. So, devil, you just take it back where it came from. This disease does not belong in my body because I am saved. And, because I am saved, I am healed, delivered, protected, preserved, and made whole in the name of Jesus. Jesus suffered every disease on the cross so I wouldn't have to."

We are not denying the fact that something is there, but rather denying the right for it to remain. So, as you can see, this is an entirely different kind of confession, and there is nothing carnal or earthly about it. It has its origins with God Himself, and He encourage us to use it in everything that we do.

Confession, Faith, and Possession

Your faith can never get past your level of confession. This is the reason Jesus said, *"According to your faith be it unto you"* (Matthew 9:29). Faith and confession go hand in hand. If your level of faith is such that you believe that you will never do anything for God because of your past sins and failures, then you won't. If your level of confession is, "My mother was on welfare and my grandmother too. My mother had kids out of wedlock, and it looks like I'm going to fall into the same trap," then this is right where you will stay. You have to rise above how the devil makes you feel and think about yourself, and that is why you must know what the Word of God teaches.

Although I was raised poor (one of seven children whose father earned fifty dollars a week) and had very few of life's amenities growing up, that didn't matter to me because of the positive confession my daddy had given me all of my life. He had said that God's hand was on me and that He was going to use me, and because I believed it, that changed everything for me. It didn't matter to me that I was probably the worse dressed girl in my high school because I knew that I would one day prosper. I didn't care how poor I was because I knew it wouldn't be long before I would be on top and no longer on the bottom.

Despite my poor dress, I kept company with the most popular students in school. This, despite the fact that I was the only girl in my gym class who had no gym shoes and had to play in her socks. I didn't care because my confession was already on another level. I knew who I was and where I was going in life.

I quit high school in the eleventh grade to marry my husband Lawrence. Although he would eventually prosper as a businessman and then as a pastor, we were poor. He bought me an old retired taxi cab to drive. The floor was rusted out of it, and it had no heat or defroster. But I didn't care. I drove that old cab with pride because I knew who I was.

When we had our first child, I would wrap her up in a blanket, scrape the frost off of the windows with my fingernails, and go visit my mother. As I drove about in that old taxi, I could already picture myself driving a Cadillac. When one of them would pass, I would say, "I'm going to drive one of those one day."

I didn't know what a Mercedes looked like, but when I saw a really nice car passing, I would say, "One day I'm going to have one of those."

When I passed a big, beautiful house, I would say, "One day I'm going to have a big, beautiful house like that."

I was able to confess these things because I knew that my heavenly Father owned it all, and today I have everything that I confessed in those days—and much more. This can be your testimony, too, if you'll get out of the stupor you're in and start believing and confessing the promises of God for your life.

You can be free of the pain you have suffered for so long. You can get out of that impossible situation you're in. Just look at yourself in the mirror and tell yourself, "You need to know who you are and start declaring it." There is power in declaration.

When I confess something, my heart, or mind, is expressing itself through the words of my lips. Confession is faith's way of expressing itself. I confess my faith through my mouth. This is the reason we need to keep company with people who speak what we speak.

Avoiding Negativity

If the people we keep company with don't speak what we speak, then we need to invite them to come up to our level of confession, and if they are unwilling to come up to our level of confession, then we need to let them go. Companionship tends to have either a redeeming or a corrupting value. Learn to fellowship with people who can propel you into your destiny.

If your present companions are speaking things that are not beneficial, gossip and innuendos, or simply negativity, tell them that you must politely refuse to participate.

Don't even speak negatively about your family members. A woman called me recently and said, "I'm afraid that my son is going to overdose on drugs."

"You're speaking it," I replied. "Is that where your faith is? Are you believing for your son to overdose on drugs? Make your confession, 'You can't kill my boy, because he is destined for greatness in the Kingdom of God. Right now, he's just out there creating a testimony that will bring many into the Kingdom.' "

Avoiding negativity is demonstrating faith. Faith is like love; it has to be demonstrated, and that is done through making a positive confession and avoiding a negative one. You can tell someone you love them, but you'd better demonstrate it too. And faith, just as love, is only revealed in your actions. There is no faith apart from confession, and your positive faith requires a positive confession.

Stop Cursing Your Children and Your Spouse

This is why it is so important what we tell our children. Confess greatness to them. Too many of us have been guilty of bringing curses upon our children by saying things like, "You'll be just like your sorry daddy. I know you have bad habits like him already. You're going to turn out just like him in every other way." If you're not careful, that son will meet your expectations, turning out to be just what you had hoped he would *not* be. Don't be guilty of speaking negative things over your children—ever.

I was speaking with a lady about some bad news coming out of North Korea about their nuclear capabilities, and we were exploring the possibility that at some moment Russia would join North Korea in war against the United States. She said that it was a biblical prophecy and that we were standing on the threshold of the coming of the Lord.

"Even so, come, Lord Jesus," I said, as had John the Revelator before me (see Revelation 22:20).

"Oh, don't say that," the woman replied. "My children are still lost."

"Don't *you* say *that,*" I responded. "If you confess that your children are lost, then lost children is what you have. You should confess, 'My children are already in the Kingdom.' Then the Lord will not come until your children get into the Kingdom. This is why I say, 'Come, Lord Jesus!' because before He comes my whole family will be saved." I not only believe it; I confess it on a regular basis.

If your husband is a "no account," "no good," "sorry thing," the reason may be that every time he comes home drinking you speak death to him—and not life. If you have said things like, "You will never amount to anything," you must repent and ask God to help you never say those things again. When your tongue expresses those sentiments, you are speaking death over his life. Don't say things like that—ever.

If your husband comes home staggering and with no clue as to where he is at the moment, say to him, "You mighty man of God. You're coming out of this. The enemy can't have what belongs to me. You are my man, the father of my children, and you will be whole." When you say words like these, you are creating the man you want. Your life follows your words.

> *Your confession opens a door, either for God to work or for Satan to work.*

Your Confession Opens a Door, and a Negative Confession Robs God of His Glory

Do you ever wonder why you always need to borrow money before your next paycheck comes? It's because this is what you are always confessing. You need to change your confession. Your confession is robbing you. The next time you get paid, you need to say, "This paycheck is more than enough to cover my needs. I can pay my tithes and give an offering to the church, and then God will help me to meet all of my current bills."

Your confession opens a door, either for God to work or for the enemy to work. Whose words are you repeating? Are your words full of faith? Or are they full of doubt and unbelief?

Your negative confession not only robs you; it robs God of His glory. He said:

YOUR LIFE FOLLOWS YOUR WORDS

Ye have ROBBED me. But ye say, Wherein have we ROBBED thee? In tithes and offerings.   Malachi 3:8

I used to think that this meant people were taking money out of God's pocket, but it didn't take me long to figure out that God didn't need any of our money. When you don't give, you're not robbing God of money; you're robbing Him of the privilege of meeting your needs. If you pay your tithes, He receives glory through blessing you in return. He longs to do it, and He is just waiting for you to start confessing it and living it. Your life follows your words.

The Power of Life and Death Is in the Tongue

It should be clear where I am going with this. Words of life and death are in our mouths:

DEATH and LIFE are IN THE POWER OF THE TONGUE.
Proverbs 18:21

Because this is true, we must choose to speak life and not death in order to reap life and not death. We must speak blessing and not cursing, if we want blessing and not cursing. I don't imagine we will ever realize in this life how very powerful our words are or how much authority is given to a very unruly member of our bodies—the tongue. James wrote of it:

My brethren, be not many masters, knowing that we shall receive the greater condemnation. For in many things we offend all. If any man offend not IN WORD, the same is a perfect man, and able also to bridle the whole body.
Behold, we put bits in the horses' mouths, that they may obey

38

us; and we turn about their whole body. Behold also the ships, which though they be so great, and are driven of fierce winds, yet are they turned about with a very small helm, whithersoever the governor listeth. Even so THE TONGUE is a little member, and boasteth great things. Behold, how great a matter a little fire kindleth! And THE TONGUE is a fire, a world of iniquity: so is THE TONGUE among our members, that it defileth the whole body, and setteth on fire the course of nature; and it is set on fire of hell.

For every kind of beasts, and of birds, and of serpents, and of things in the sea, is tamed, and hath been tamed of mankind: But THE TONGUE can no man tame; it is an unruly evil, full of deadly poison.

Therewith bless we God, even the Father; and therewith curse we men, which are made after the similitude of God. Out of the same MOUTH proceedeth blessing and cursing. My brethren, these things ought not so to be. Doth a fountain send forth at the same place sweet water and bitter? Can the fig tree, my brethren, bear olive berries? either a vine, figs? so can no fountain both yield salt water and fresh.

Who is a wise man and endued with knowledge among you? let him show out of a good CONVERSATION his works with meekness of wisdom.   James 3:1-13

Who can tame the tongue? Who can keep it from speaking negativity? Who can keep it from speaking words that bring a curse down upon us? God has set before us life and death and gives us the option to choose. How can we choose life? By speaking it. We confess what we choose, and this determines what we will possess.

James said we have not because we ask not, and Jesus said that we must speak to a mountain if we want it to move. They were both teaching us the power of our words.

YOUR LIFE FOLLOWS YOUR WORDS

Many people insist, "I never speak what I want; I just believe it." I'm sorry, but your desire will never come to fruition until you actually verbalize it. There is something very powerful about speaking out the promises of the Word of God.

Be Careful What You Say

God's Word declares:

> *For by thy WORDS thou shalt be JUSTIFIED, and by thy WORDS thou shalt be CONDEMNED.* Matthew 12:37

There is something very powerful about speaking out the promises of the Word of God.

When you stand at the Judgment Seat, it will be your words that will justify you. If you don't make the Rapture (those of you who are without Christ), it will be because of your words. They will have condemned you. Choose to say what God says.

In Chapter 5 we will deal more with how to deal with a tongue bent on making wrong confessions. God knows we have all made enough of them. A wrong confession is one that voices defeat and failure. Christians do it—even in public. I have noticed that when we invite people to give their testimonies in public, it is very difficult for them not to glamorize the devil in the process. One brother noticed my dismay at his testimony and asked me if he was out of order.

"You surely are," I had to reply. "We don't brag on our defeats, our failures, our confusion, and our fear. That's 'junk' that doesn't need to be told. When you speak of how the enemy is controlling your life, keeping you down, and keeping you sick, you are glorifying him. When you say, 'I've been so bad off lately,' the imps in hell rejoice and exclaim, "Yeah! We've got him now by his own words!"

When we talk about the devil's work in our lives, we are making an unconscious declaration that God is a failure and that the Word of God is not true. Unconsciously we are saying, "God has failed me because I'm sick, because I'm in need, because I'm fearful, or because I'm down." A great majority of our words give glory to Satan and, in the process, they destroy our faith and hold us in bondage.

As long as you hold fast to your confession of weakness, sickness, and pain, you will have it. You may search for years for a Benny Hinn, an Oral Roberts, or some other faith healer to pray for you— to no avail—because your unbelief will destroy the positive effect of *any* man or woman's faith. You might blame the fact that you don't get healed on the man or woman of God, but it's not them that's at fault; it's your confession. You must realize what you are doing to yourself and change your confession,

Healing and Confession—The Body Responds to the Mind

The reason confession is so important to healing is that your body responds to your mind (or spirit). Then your mind can gain lordship over your body, and the body begins to obey the confession that comes from your mind. Science has proven this fact over and over. The mind always controls the body.

When you speak what your mind believes, your body hears your words and responds. And these words make you do things you couldn't do before they were spoken.

One of my brothers used this principal on me when we were younger—in a negative way. He would bet the girls in our school that I could beat them in a fight. I didn't have a reason to be fighting with any of them, but my brother would say, "Darlene, Honey, you're a Gabbard. You may be little, but nobody can whip you when you get mad."

Because he said that nobody would beat me, I thought it was the truth, and when a girl would come up to me and start pulling my hair and saying, "Your brother said you could whip me," I would answer, "I can," and I would. It didn't matter how big the girl was; I beat her in the ensuing fight. In fact, I "whipped" every girl that tried it.

Daddy had done the same thing, but in a positive way. After I had heard his positive confession enough times, nothing could discourage me. I knew that one day I was coming out of poverty. I had made my daddy's confession my own and knew that God had something great for me. This changed the way I talked and the way I acted.

Without us realizing it, confession affects us internally. Every word we speak is a seed that is sown and will one day bear fruit:

> *A man's belly shall be satisfied with the fruit of his MOUTH; and with the increase of his LIPS shall he be filled.*
>
> Proverbs 18:20

Stop Repeating the Enemy's Lies

It is evident that most of us have not yet come to appreciate the fact that the power of life and death lie in our tongues because we say what the enemy says. We repeat his lies:

> *I can't pay my car note, and they're going to be sending someone to repossess it.*

The Necessary Confession

We say things like this only because we are ignorant of what the Word of God says. We don't know what the truth is about our confession, so we have nothing to stand on. This is a message that we need to preach over and over again in our churches. If our people can get hold of this, we won't need a prayer line in every service. We won't need the church to subsidize the finances of our members. Through their faith and confession, they will be able to receive what God has already provided for them. They will walk in health, able to get up in the morning and say, "Arthritis, you can't stay in my knee."

As we adopt God's thinking, we gradually change the way we talk, and the way we talk determines our future. Then, we are able to walk in what we believe.

Make God's Promises Personal

There are thousands of promises in the Word of God that we can confess, but the important thing is to make them your own. For instance, if the enemy tries to put fear on you, you can confess:

> *For God hath not given us the SPIRIT OF FEAR; but of power, and of love, and of a sound mind.*　　　　2 Timothy 1:7

Now make it personal. Say:

> *God has not given ME the spirit of fear, but of power, and love, and a sound mind. Therefore, thanks be to God, I fear no evil.*

Do this same thing with every promise of God. It may have been spoken to Israel, but it was prophetically yours as well.

One of the things we all love about the Twenty-Third Psalm is that it *is* so personal and needs no rewording to mean just what we need it to mean at this very moment and in the particular crisis each of us finds ourselves in:

> *The LORD is MY shepherd; I shall not want.*
>
> *He maketh ME to lie down in green pastures: he leadeth ME beside the still waters.*
>
> *He restoreth MY soul: he leadeth ME in the paths of righteousness for his name's sake.*
>
> *Yea, though I walk through the valley of the shadow of death, I will fear no evil: for thou art with ME; thy rod and thy staff they comfort ME.*
>
> *Thou preparest a table before ME in the presence of MINE enemies: thou anointest MY head with oil; MY cup runneth over.*
>
> *Surely goodness and mercy shall follow ME all the days of MY life: and I will dwell in the house of the LORD for ever.*
>
> Psalm 23:1-6

In the face of every need, we must confess that He is our Shepherd, and that He is our Shepherd now. (See more on the timing of our confession in Chapter 7). Believe in your heart and confess with your mouth that every word in the Bible is true, that it is full of power, and that it can change your situation. Jesus said:

> *Behold, I give unto YOU power to tread on serpents and scorpions, and over all the power of the enemy: and nothing shall by any means hurt YOU.* Luke 10:19

That is about as personal as you can get. This word *power* means the ability to make good. So, when Jesus said, *"I give you all power over all the power of the enemy"* [my paraphrase], He was saying that you have the power, or ability, to make good every circumstance in life the enemy meant for evil through your confession of the Word of God. This is the reason that no weapon formed against you will prosper:

> *No weapon that is formed against THEE shall prosper; and every tongue that shall rise against THEE in judgment thou shalt condemn. This is the heritage of the servants of the LORD, and their righteousness is of me, saith the LORD.*
>
> Isaiah 54:17

Again, make it personal, and know that God meant it for you:

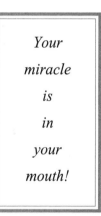

Your miracle is in your mouth!

> *No weapon that is formed against ME shall prosper; and every tongue that shall rise against ME in judgment I shall condemn. This is MY heritage in the Lord, and MY righteousness is of Him, saith the LORD.*

The Bible was not written for other people but for YOU. Just as surely as Christ would have died on Calvary if you had been the only person alive to need His salvation, He would have given His Word if you were the only person alive who needed it. It is yours; make it that.

Here's another promise that we love because it is so personal:

> *I can do all things through Christ which strengtheneth me.*
>
> Philippians 4:13

"I..." I can do all things. And I can do all things because Christ strengthens ME.

You may be among those who lack education, but if you have

Christ you can do all things. You may be among those who have never enjoyed a proportional share of life's goods, but if you have Christ, you can do all things. You may be among those who have had difficulty finding a good church home and have suffered the lack of a good pastor and caring brothers and sisters. But if you have Christ, you can do all things. You and I can live this Christian life and can one day see our Lord face to face because we have victory through His name. Nothing can hinder us if we have Christ. Let that be your confession today.

Visualize It and Then Confess It

Much has been written about the ability to visualize ourselves in God's perfect will, and using that as a tool of faith to achieve our spiritual goals. This is a powerful tool indeed. I would carry it one step further. After you have visualized it, then confess it.

Begin to see yourself healed and healthy. Those of you who now confess that you have arthritis, picture yourself as the choir leader dancing energetically before God with no pain. Picture yourself running through the aisles of your church praising God. Get a vision of yourself healed, delivered, protected, preserved, and made whole because you are saved.

See yourself with the new job you so desperately need. Put yourself in the new car you have been wanting. Picture yourself with a new house. Picture yourself with your spouse on fire for God, working in the church. Picture yourself with your children all saved. Think about how it will feel to have the whole salvation package. Visualize it, and then start confessing it. Now begin to praise God for it.

Your miracle is in your mouth, and when you begin to confess your miracle with your mouth, then you can also begin to give thanks unto God. And, when people ask you how you are doing, tell them your confession. Tell them, "I am wonderful because I am saved, healed, delivered, protected, preserved, and made whole."

Some of you may be wondering, "What if they reply, 'Well you don't look healed' and walk off thinking I am crazy?" Just know that they won't think you are crazy very long—especially when you get your next doctor's report.

As you learn to put into words God's desire for your life and make those desires your own, you will be ready to pray with power and authority the prayer of faith and see the sick delivered and raised up.

Chapter 3

THE NECESSARY FAITH

But without faith it is impossible to please him: for he that cometh to God must believe that he is, and that he is a rewarder of them that diligently seek him.　　　　Hebrews 11:6

The prayer of faith is just that—a prayer *"of faith."* There is an element of faith that we must understand and rise to if we are to bring healing to those who are in need.

Early in my revisit of the healing promises of the Bible, the Lord reminded me that His Word can conquer any evil and, therefore, any sickness, but He also reminded me that His Word must be activated by faith if we are to realize any of its benefits. Without faith, we cannot even please God. A lack of faith will keep us from receiving salvation from sin, and a lack of faith will keep us from receiving the other benefits of salvation, including healing.

The Law of Faith

When I preach on healing these days, I start with the fact that our world is governed by laws. For instance, there is the Law of Gravity. While this law, actually known as the Universal Law of Gravitation, is quite complex and technical in Isaac Newton's original statement of it, most of us understand it to mean that when an object is released, it falls to the ground. According to dictionary.com, gravity can be defined as: "The natural force of attraction exerted by a celestial body, such as Earth, upon objects at or near its surface, tending to draw them toward the center of the body. That's why things fall when they are released.

Most people understand the Law of Gravity, having experienced it since they were small children, and so if they jump from a tall building, they should expect to hurt themselves. That's just the way gravity works. Our world is governed by the laws of physics, and we must abide by those laws if we are to function normally in it.

> *A rhema word is a word spoken directly by God to you or me for a specific situation.*

When we are born again into the spiritual world, there are others laws, laws that the world is ignorant of, and we must learn to abide by these laws of the Spirit. These are set into the Body of Christ. There are laws, principles and precepts, and if we are to receive the thirty thousand promises of God's Word, we must learn to obey these laws, principles, and precepts. The Law of Faith is the most important of these, and without it, we can receive nothing from God.

What Is Faith?

What is faith? In its simplest terms, faith is believing. It is trusting in, relying upon, or confiding in someone or something. In the case of the Lord, we believe His testimony to be sure because He has never failed. He has proven Himself to be absolutely trustworthy. It is not hard to have faith in God.

We have faith in some people (because they have proven to be totally trustworthy), and we have absolutely no faith in others (because they have proven to be totally untrustworthy). Thank goodness that faith in people is not required for salvation, only faith in God.

This faith *is* required. We *"must believe,"* as the writer of the book of Hebrews stated, and there are two things that we *"must believe"* in order to move toward salvation: (1) *"that he is,"* and (2) *"that he is a rewarder of them that diligently seek him."* This is the necessary process, believing that God exists and that He is the Savior, but also that His salvation is for me and that He will reward me with it as I seek Him. Most Christians understand this part of faith, because they have experienced it.

The surprise comes to many new Christians, when they have taken up their confession and picked up their cross, and suddenly they are faced with problems they have never faced before. This is because they are now fighting their spiritual enemy, the very one whom they formerly served, and he is determined to destroy their souls and drag them down to hell.

When this happens, new believers should realize that something more is needed. They have believed the incarnate Word of God, and it has brought them to Him, but now they need a more specific word, what we in the Church world have come to call a *rhema* word. A *rhema* word is a word spoken directly by God to you or me for a specific situation. We all need such a word to sustain us in our day-to-day walk with the Lord, and we must exercise faith in that specific word from the Lord, just as we must exercise faith in His written and eternal Word.

How Do We Get Faith?

Another question I asked myself as I reviewed the process of developing an effective *"prayer of faith"* was how does faith come to us? The Scriptures offer an answer to that question:

YOUR LIFE FOLLOWS YOUR WORDS

*So then faith cometh by hearing, and hearing by the word of
God.*   Romans 10:17

Faith is something that no one can teach us to have, and neither
can we teach others to have it. We either believe, or we don't believe. What we *can* teach others is how to hear the Word of God so
that their capacity to believe can be enlarged. This happens in three
steps: INSPIRATION, REVELATION, AND ILLUMINATION. Let
me explain how this works.

The first thing that happens when we hear the Word of God is
that we are inspired. Revelation comes when that inspired Word is
quickened, or made alive. And finally, when the meaning of the
word is made known to you and you realize that it is specifically for
you, this is illumination. It is the understanding that the Scriptures
are not just words written on paper, but that the word revealed to
me is for my unique situation, and that I am to take hold of it and
stand on it until it becomes reality.

Paul wrote to the Ephesian believers:

*That the God of our Lord Jesus Christ, the Father of glory, may
give unto you the spirit of wisdom and REVELATION in the
knowledge of him: the eyes of your understanding being EN-
LIGHTENED; that ye may know what is the hope of his calling,
and what the riches of the glory of his inheritance in the saints,
and what is the exceeding greatness of his power to us-ward
who believe.*   Ephesians 1:17-18

The writer to the Hebrews explained it this way:

*But call to remembrance the former days, in which after ye were
ILLUMINATED, ye endured a great fight of afflictions.*
                                                    Hebrews 10:32

Once you get inspired revelation that has been illuminated, you don't have to wait for the physical manifestation of it before you can begin to praise God. You can go ahead and act on it. I can start praising God immediately because I know that what He has said is true and will come to pass.

I have grasped the thing in faith, and that faith becomes the actual material, the *"substance,"* or physical matter, for which I am believing, and *"the evidence"* that I have what I am believing for—although I cannot yet see it:

> *Now faith is the SUBSTANCE of things hoped for, the EVIDENCE of things not seen.* Hebrews 11:1

So the prayer of faith is a prayer of substance. It is a prayer for something you cannot see, and yet you believe that you already have it. You already have the evidence of it, and that evidence comes to you through the revelation, inspiration, and illumination of the Holy Ghost.

Abraham As An Example

Abraham, the father of our faith, knew what it was to pray the prayer of faith. He had tapped into something that we could all use. Among his many exploits in faith, he was able to believe God for a son he could not yet father, and he could do that because he believed what God had said about his future. Therefore, the Scriptures say of him:

> *(As it is written, I have made thee a father of many nations,) before him whom he believed, even God, who quickeneth the dead, and calleth those things which be not as though they were.* Romans 4:17

Abraham learned to reach into the future through the promise of God and his faith in that promise and to pull into the present that which God had said would be his. In this way, he learned to call those things that were not as though they were. This is exactly what we must do when we pray the prayer of faith. We must speak of things that do not yet exist as though they did. This is the mark of a true believer.

What Is A Believer?

What is a believer? In the most common usage, we speak of believers as those who have accepted Jesus as their Lord and Savior. In other words, they have believed on Him for initial salvation. But our believing in the Lord, and thus, our life as believers, should go much further. In a greater sense, a believer is one who is convinced that he has in the physical realm exactly what he is hoping for in the spiritual realm. He is able to call things that are not as though they were, to speak of what does not yet exist as though it did. As a result, it does.

This kind of believing always produces results. When we believe for salvation from sins, we are saved from sins. When we believe for healing, we are healed. When we believe for miracles, they happen. Whatever you believe for will come your way. You will bring it out of the realm of future possibility and into the realm of present reality by your faith.

Who Can Believe?

Another important question related to the prayer of faith is who can believe? The ability to believe is not necessarily a divine ability. People can believe a lie and be damned because of it. Some believe in and serve the false gods of this world. You can believe literally anything you want. So anyone can believe, but not everyone believes the truth.

In order to exercise the prayer of faith, our belief must be focused on the Savior, the Healer and Miracle Worker, and on the fact that His benefits are for us. For the salvation of the soul, we must become convinced that the Word of our God is true, that Jesus is the Son of God, that He is the only way to the Father, and that this salvation is for us. For the salvation of the body, we must believe His promises concerning healing and divine health and that they are for us. And for the prosperity that is intended to be a major part of our salvation, we must believe God's promises concerning the fact that He is our Father, that He loves us more than we can ever know, and that His desire is to lavish us with good gifts.

> *A believer is one who is convinced that he has in the physical realm exactly what he is hoping for in the spiritual realm.*

Although faith is neither good nor bad (we choose to direct our faith toward the right or the wrong), true faith is a grace from God. That is, He gives us the ability to believe that what He says is true.

So who can believe? Actually, we all have a *"measure of faith"*:

God hath dealt to every man the measure of faith.

Romans 12:3

Even sinners have this measure of faith, for the measure of faith is given to every man by God to enable us to believe in something we cannot see. His hope is that we will believe on Him and be saved. If this element of common faith did not exist, no man could even come to God.

YOUR LIFE FOLLOWS YOUR WORDS

The responsibility, then, of believing rests on the individual. We have been given a measure of faith, and it is up to us to develop that measure we have been given. It is up to us to become a true believer in Christ. Once we become a believer, we must begin to take what is unseen and speak of it as already seen, take the promises of the future and bring them into the present, call that which is not as though it were.

Faith is not always found where we expect it to be. For instance, on several occasions, when His disciples had failed to overcome the circumstances around them (for instance, when they encountered a storm at sea and were frightened), Jesus asked them:

Where is your faith?   Luke 8:25

The problem was not with the Lord or with His promise of care for His disciples. The problem was their fear, their doubt, their unbelief. The prayer of faith, without the faith, is just another prayer, and when we pray without faith, we cannot expect our prayers to save the sick or for the Lord to raise them up.

Then, sometimes we find faith where we least expect it. A Gentile woman brought her daughter to Jesus for healing. Because of who she was, at first He didn't even answer her. He was sent to *"the lost sheep of the house of Israel,"* He said (Matthew 15:24), and it was not right to *"take the children's bread, and to cast it to dogs"* (verse 26). When she responded that she was willing to *"eat the crumbs"* that fell from His table, Jesus recognized her faith and healed her daughter. What he said to the woman that day is quite amazing:

Then Jesus answered and said unto her, O WOMAN, GREAT IS THY FAITH: BE IT UNTO THEE EVEN AS THOU WILT. And her daughter was made whole from that very hour.
                                                    Matthew 15:28

The Necessary Faith

This woman from a pagan background received what she was seeking because she believed that the Lord was willing and able to do it. If we can believe, how much more will He do for us, far beyond what we are asking Him for:

> *Now unto him that is able to do exceeding abundantly ABOVE ALL THAT WE ASK OR THINK, according to the power that worketh in us ...*   Ephesians 3:20

It's all waiting for our positive response to God and His Word.

How Much Faith Does It Take?

So how much faith does it take to pray an effective prayer of healing? It must not take much because Jesus said that if we had faith the size of a grain of mustard seed, we would have power to move mountains:

> *Verily I say unto you, If ye have faith as a grain of mustard seed, ye shall say unto this mountain, Remove hence to yonder place; and it shall remove; and NOTHING SHALL BE IM-POSSIBLE UNTO YOU.*   Matthew 17:20

My what a powerful promise, and it is the result of faith *"as a grain of mustard seed."*

Mustard seeds are very tiny, so it doesn't take much faith, and we already have some. I can't say how much faith the Lord gave us when He gave us *"the measure of faith,"* that measure we needed in order to be saved. But as our faith grows through hearing the Word of God, we should easily be able to come to the level of faith necessary to pray the prayer of faith and see ourselves and others healed.

Hoping Against Hope

One of the most important elements of faith is perseverance, hoping against hope. Paul wrote of Abraham:

Who against hope believed in hope, that he might become the father of many nations, according to that which was spoken, So shall thy seed be.   Romans 4:18

> *It made no difference to Abraham that his body was already "dead."*

What did Paul mean when he said that Abraham *"against hope believed in hope"*? He meant that everything was against him, but he believed anyway. This bold faith made Abraham *"the father of many nations."* It happened, not because Abraham was great, but because God was great. He had spoken and said, *"So shall thy seed be,"* and Abraham believed that God was trustworthy. He believed what God said—even when his circumstances said otherwise:

And being not weak in faith, he considered not his own body now dead, when he was about an hundred years old, neither yet the deadness of Sarah's womb.   Romans 4:19

It made no difference to Abraham that his body was already *"dead."* His circumstances didn't change God. If God had said that he would be the father of many nations, then it would come to pass—regardless of the circumstances. Abraham believed it, and therefore it would become reality in his life. He began to pull the future into the present by calling those things that were not as though they were, and it happened. God had spoken of things that were not yet manifested, and Abraham chose to believe them ... until they *were* manifested.

God gave His promises to Abraham several times. Although Abraham believed what he heard God speak the very first time, every time he heard it again, his faith increased. Speaking out what we are believing for, therefore, causes our faith to increase. Faith comes by hearing the Word of God, and you might as well be the one to speak it.

Abraham was *"not weak in faith,"* even though he was *"about an hundred years old"* already. Now that's faith! This man refused to entertain the fact that he was impotent (and they had no Viagra or other such drug in his day to help him). He even refused to consider the fact that Sarah was already well past the age for childbearing.

God had said they would have a child, and that was all Abraham could consider. It was all he *wanted* to consider. He purposely shut out all other thoughts and kept his mind focused on that one thing ... until it became reality. In this way, he was *"strong in faith."*

Being *"Strong in Faith"*

He staggered not at the promise of God through unbelief; but was STRONG IN FAITH, giving glory to God.
Romans 4:20

The original Greek gives us the sense that Abraham began to praise God for the blessing even before it happened. And that is exactly what we need to do. If we are to bring the future into the present and speak of things that are not as though they were, it's as good as done, and we can start praising God for it.

The prayer of faith is a prayer of rejoicing. Because we believe what God has said and are willing to confess it and to stand on that confession, we can begin to praise Him even before the victory is manifested. Continue praising God until you receive the full manifestation. And as you praise God, remember to continue to call those things that are not yet manifested as though they were.

This is the point at which many of us get into trouble. We whine and complain about our circumstances, and we fail to praise God in advance for the manifestation of His promise. And what does this indicate to God? Praising Him in advance is a sign of faith on our part, and whining and complaining is a sign of doubt and unbelief. And praising so delights God that He lavishes us with gifts.

When we worship Him, He takes the things He has stored up for us, puts them into a mighty heap and then pours them down upon us. This begins to happen even while we are in the midst of worshiping. He says to us:

> *There's the healing you have been needing.*
> *There's the financial breakthrough you asked Me for.*
> *There's salvation for your children.*
> *There's some more peace and contentment.*

He has promised to open up the windows of heaven and pour us out a blessing that we cannot even contain:

> **Prove me now herewith, saith the LORD of hosts, if I will not open you the windows of heaven, and pour you out a blessing, that THERE SHALL NOT BE ROOM ENOUGH TO RECEIVE IT.** Malachi 3:10

Imagine so many blessings that you have to give some of them away. Such blessings come to those who believe God enough to worship Him in advance for the answer.

Therefore, every time we receive a promise from God, we should go ahead and praise Him, even as we hold fast to the promise and believe for its fulfillment. To do this, of course, you must be *"fully persuaded."*

Being *"Fully Persuaded"*

Abraham was *"fully persuaded"* in his heart:

> **And being FULLY PERSUADED that, what he had promised, he was able also to perform.** Romans 4:21

Abraham was not like a lot of us. He didn't wake up one morning saying that God was going to do it and then wake up the next morning saying, "I can't see how God will do this thing. After all, just look at our bodies. What do you think God really meant by what He said? Surely He didn't mean it literally. I don't think He can 'pull off' what we thought He was saying He would do."

That sounds like many of us, but Abraham was *"fully persuaded."* If God had promised it, then it would come, for God *"was able also to perform [it]."* Abraham didn't try to figure out how it would happen; he just believed that it would. After all, God had proven Himself to be trustworthy again and again.

Are you *"fully persuaded"* today? You can be.

Ignoring the Circumstances

Abraham is a great example of someone who prayed the proper prayer of faith because the words he spoke were consistent with his desire. He determined to speak words of faith concerning his situation and to ignore the circumstances. Most believers today do just the opposite. We pray many of our prayers out of unbelief:

Oh, God! I've got cancer, and I'm afraid I won't live to raise my children.

Oh, God! I'm afraid I'm about to lose my job, and then I'll never prosper as You promised.

God, My marriage seems to be failing, and I don't know what to do about it.

These are very typical of our prayers. They express fear, doubt, and a total respect for the circumstances. But if we really believe God, we will not even consider the circumstances or the situation. We will simply repeat God's words, saying what He has said, knowing that He will change whatever has to be changed to bring it to pass. Those who cannot look over their current circumstances to see the coming victory will never receive it. They are doomed to struggle on with the cares of life.

Faith Makes All Things Possible

Jesus said that if we could believe, all things would be possible to us:

> *Jesus said unto him, If thou canst believe, ALL THINGS ARE POSSIBLE TO HIM THAT BELIEVETH.*   Mark 9:23

There is nothing God cannot do—if we abide in His Word and believe Him for it. So if there is an unfulfilled desire in our lives it is because there is a root of unbelief lurking somewhere in our hearts. God provided for the fulfillment of all our desires two thousand years ago, and the prayer of faith will bring forth the manifestation of it—if we can learn the various important elements of that prayer and put them into practice.

Faith and Confession

As we noted in the previous chapter, our faith grows with our confession. You might say, "I'm healed," and your faith will grow from a seed to a blade. If you say, "I know I'm healed," your faith will grow a little more, from a blade to a stalk. When you say more boldly, "I feel healed," your faith will grow even more, from a stalk to an ear. Until finally God will say, "That's all you need. You have what you are believing Me for," and the *"full ear"* will become evident:

> *There is nothing God cannot do—if we abide in His Word and believe Him for it.*

For the earth bringeth forth fruit of herself; first the blade, then the ear, after that the full corn in the ear.   Mark 4:28

Always remember that faith never grows beyond your confession. If you can't believe it, you can't receive it. And if you can't say it, you can't have it. Your daily confession of what the spirit is doing in you will build a positive, solid faith life. You will not be afraid of any circumstance that comes to your life because you know you are saved, healed, delivered, protected, preserved, and made whole. You will face life fearlessly because you are a conqueror, a King's kid.

When you have stepped into a new level of faith, you are ready to pray the prayer known by that name—the prayer of faith.

Chapter 4

THE NECESSARY RIGHT THINKING

If ye then, being evil, know how to give good gifts unto your children, how much more shall your Father which is in heaven give good things to them that ask him? Matthew 7:11

The prayer of faith is a prayer of right thinking, and until we get our thinking straight, we cannot pray this prayer effectively.

Understanding Our Heavenly Father and His Love For Us

Much of the problem with our thinking is that we don't really understand God, His goodness, His greatness, His unlimited ability, His unmatched love for us as His children, and what that all means to us personally.

When a child is born into a natural family, it is the understood responsibility of the father in that family to care for the child. This includes providing food and clothing, shelter and protection, and a whole lot more. Fathers take on a lot when they decide to bring a child into this world.

As with any other responsibility to a child, when a child becomes ill, it is the understood responsibility of the father to get the child well as quickly as possible—whatever has to be done. Many men are very good at the duties of fatherhood, but even the best fathers could never be compared with our Father God. He is the very best father any of us could ever ask for or hope to have.

God is far more responsible than any earthly father, and it is His job to perfect everything that concerns me simply because He is my Father:

> *The Lord will perfect THAT WHICH CONCERNETH ME.*
>
> Psalm 138:8

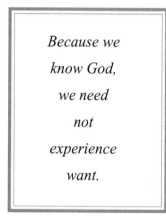

Because we know God, we need not experience want.

It is God's responsibility to be my Savior. It is His responsibility to be my Healer. It is His responsibility to be my Deliverer, my Protector, my Preserver, and the provider of my wholeness. The Bible shows that He does more than any earthly father could— *"HOW MUCH MORE"!*

God gives very good things to His children. He has promised us food, shelter, and clothing:

> *Therefore I say unto you, Take no thought for your life, what ye shall EAT, or what ye shall DRINK; nor yet for your body, what ye shall PUT ON. Is not the life more than meat, and the body than raiment? Behold the fowls of the air: for they sow not, neither do they reap, nor gather into barns; yet your heavenly Father feedeth them. Are ye not much better than they? Which of you by taking thought can add one cubit unto his stature? And why take ye thought for raiment? Consider the lilies of the field, how they grow; they toil not, neither do they spin: and yet I say unto you, That even Solomon in all his glory was not arrayed like one of these. Wherefore, if God so clothe the grass of*

The Necessary Right Thinking

the field, which to day is, and to morrow is cast into the oven,
shall he not much more clothe you, O ye of little faith? There-
fore take no thought, saying, What shall we EAT? or, What
shall we DRINK? or, Wherewithal shall we be CLOTHED?
(For after all these things do the Gentiles seek:) for your heav-
enly Father knoweth that ye have need of ALL THESE THINGS.
But seek ye first the kingdom of God, and his righteousness;
and all these things SHALL BE ADDED UNTO YOU.

Matthew 6:25-33

Because we know God, we need not experience want.

God, our heavenly Father, also sends angels to protect us and keep us in *"all [our] ways":*

For he shall give his angels charge over thee, TO KEEP THEE
in all thy ways.
They shall bear thee up in their hands, lest thou dash thy foot
against a stone.
Thou shalt tread upon the lion and adder: the young lion and
the dragon shalt thou trample under feet.
Because he hath set his love upon me, therefore will I deliver
him: I will set him on high, because he hath known my name.
He shall call upon me, and I will answer him: I will be with
him in trouble; I will deliver him, and honour him.
With long life will I satisfy him, and show him my salvation.

Psalm 91:11-16

Interestingly enough, this promise of angels to keep us *"in ALL [our] ways"* is valid whether our ways happen to be good or evil. Some of you were targets for Satan and have been shot at, and you may wonder why you're still alive. The bullets intended for you could not kill you because God assigned an angel to you to keep you—even while you were living in sin. What a good and gracious Father He is!

When others of you were so high on drugs or otherwise intoxicated while driving that you couldn't remember driving home or understand how you even got there, it was because God assigned an angel to keep you. Some have crawled into a bed laced with AIDS and wondered why you could not function normally sexually. It was because our heavenly Father gave an angel charge over you to keep you in your way.

If God would do that for those of us who are disobeying Him, how much more will He do for those who are following His will! He wants to give us more than we can even ask or think.

Clearly God wants to give us more, but He is waiting for us to understand His goodness and to ask for what is rightfully ours as His children.

Jesus said that He came to give us *"life more abundantly"*:

> **The thief cometh not, but for to steal, and to kill, and to destroy: I am come that they might have life, and that they might have it more abundantly.** John 10:10

This word *abundantly* is from the Greek word *perissos*. According to *Strongs* (#4053) it carries the meaning: "Superabundance, excessive, overflowing, surplus, over and above, more than enough, profuse, extraordinary, above the ordinary, more than sufficient." This is the Gospel Jesus preached. He came to give His children life—not merely an existence, but an overflowing, prosperous way of living. Our Father has prepared for us a wonderful and exciting journey called life.

How great I feel when I give gifts to my children. I love to do it—

especially to those who are already working in the Kingdom. And that's how God is; He *loves* to give us gifts, all kinds of gifts. We just need to get in the place that we can receive them. Based on our knowledge of who He is and of His great love for us, we can begin to make a daily confession that will change our personal lives and also make us effective in ministry to others.

The Father's Provision for Our Healing

As we saw in an earlier chapter, Isaiah spoke of our Father's provision for our healing (and every other aspect of salvation) through Christ:

> *But he was wounded for OUR transgressions, he was bruised for OUR iniquities: the chastisement of OUR peace was upon him; and with his stripes WE are healed.*   Isaiah 53:5

The Moffatt translation of the Bible renders this verse as: *"Surely He has born my sicknesses and carried my pain, and I have come to appreciate Him as the One Who was stricken, smitten of God with my diseases, and now I know that by His stripes I am healed."* You need to *know* for sure that He has born YOUR sicknesses and carried YOUR diseases in His body and that because of the stripes He suffered YOU are healed. When you know this, you can make a confession that you *are* healed—no matter what your symptoms indicate. The symptoms may not leave your body at once, but that won't matter because you have something to hold fast to. Your confession is based on God's unfailing promises.

In many churches, if someone asks how many are sick, more than half of the congregation stands. Why are so many Christians sick if Jesus has already provided for our healing? It is because we don't yet know and understand the benefits of salvation. We're healed, but we don't know it yet. We must start thinking right, and then we can talk right and act right.

What grieves the heart of God is that when His children get sick, the first thing they do is call a doctor. Thank God for good doctors. We have several who are members of Solid Rock Church. But God should always take priority over doctors. Of course, God can use a doctor even if we have faith.

Think of how God feels about us always running first to someone else. Wouldn't you also be grieved if every time your child became ill he went to a neighbor for relief instead of seeking you out first for comfort and wellness? If he consulted all of the neighbors and none of them could help him, and he finally came to you as a last resort and asked, "Daddy/Mama, can you help me?", how would you feel about that?

This is how we treat our Father God. When our marriages are in trouble, for example, we call a psychologist or professional marriage counselor and plead, "Please help me. My marriage is going under."

Next, we seek out a lawyer and say, "I'm on the verge of divorce; what do you suggest I do?"

We go from here to there and from this one to that one instead of running to God's altar and proclaiming to our heavenly Father as we should, "God, I'm believing for my marriage to be restored. The devil is not taking my wife. I'm holding on to her because she's mine. You gave her to me. Now work on her and make her the woman she needs to be."

Anything less than this is a statement of unbelief, and when we don't believe our gracious and loving heavenly Father, we are calling him a liar. This breaks His heart.

Let's get our thinking right, and then the prayer of faith will do what it is supposed to do.

What You Think Is What You Are

Clearly the reason many children of God are not walking in their full inheritance is that their thinking has not yet become adjusted to, or come into alignment with, God's Word. The Scriptures teach that what we think is what we are:

For as he [a man] thinketh in his heart, so is he.

Proverbs 23:7

Many of us are still thinking the way the world thinks. Once our thinking lines up with the Word of God, we will no longer consider what the world says about a given situation.

Your doctor, for instance, may say that you have a condition in your body, but the Word of God says that when you were saved from sin, you were also healed, delivered, protected, preserved, and made whole. Which will you choose to believe?

This also goes for the drug abuser. When you were saved, you were delivered. You don't need someone to cast the devil out of you. You don't need endless drug counseling. You need to set your mind on the reality of what Jesus did for you on Calvary and start walking it out in your daily life. Take what is rightfully yours.

Would God cleanse us by His blood and then allow us to go right back into a life of bondage and pain? Surely not. So, if it happens, it's not His fault, but because of a lack of proper teaching on our part.

When we get up every morning, we should confess: "I got up this

> *Once our thinking lines up with the Word of God, we will no longer consider what the world says about a given situation.*

morning saved, and that means that I'm healed, delivered, protected, preserved, and made whole. There is not a feeble part of this body. I am more than a conqueror. Every fiber of my being is blessed. I will walk today in health, and I walk today in wealth because my soul prospers. This is true because my heavenly Father loves me so much and has made full provision for me." If you will believe it and declare it, you cannot help but prosper physically and financially, for this is our Father's will for each of us.

Rich Without Knowing It

If Christ is in you, and you are in Him, is it logical to think that God, our heavenly Father, would want you to lack something? As parents, we give everything we have to our children as—long as they are well-behaved. The only reason we would ever consider disinheriting a child is if they became disobedient and brought disgrace on the family. Otherwise, all that we have is theirs.

But if we don't know our Father's will for us, how can we claim it? An interesting story is told of a slave lady named Anna Mae who had served her owner since she was a very small girl. As her master was dying, he handed her an envelope containing a letter. Imagining that it was simply a letter of thanks for her faithful service to him through the years, she thanked him for it. But, since she could not read it, when she got home she merely fastened the envelope, with the unread letter still inside, to the wall of her quarters, and there it remained for many years.

It was only as she herself lay dying that a minister came to visit her. Curious about the envelope thumbtacked to the wall, he asked if he could look inside, and she readily gave him her permission. The minister was dumbstruck by what he read.

"Anna Mae," he said, "where did you get this letter?"

"My master gave it to me on his death bed," she answered.

"Well, do you know what it says?" he asked.

"No, sir," she replied. "I never read it, because I never learned to read or write, but I always thought that he was thanking me for all the years I took care of him and his family."

"But, Anna Mae," he cried, "this letter states that the man was leaving everything he owned to you," and he was a very wealthy man indeed.

It was a true story, and this sad commentary describes the plight of many of God's children. He has treasures set aside for us, but many never obtain them because they don't know who they are and what they possess. They don't read, they don't study, and they don't pray, and therefore they don't know what belongs to them. So they live and die in poverty and sickness, when they could have all that they need.

This is the reason the enemy wants to keep you from reading and studying the Word of God. Every time you pick it up, he tries to rock you to sleep. He tells you, "You have too much to do. Just read two or three verses and then go on to bed." It's because he doesn't want you to know who you are, what you possess, and the power you have in God.

The Process of Changing Our Minds

Many of the things we confess in prayer are said only because we are ignorant of what the Word of God says. Because we don't know the truth, we have nothing to stand on. In the very first level of our process of building faith in a loving heavenly Father, we need to include the art of meditating on His truths. Meditating is the act of thinking on the Word of God and then asking ourselves, "How can I change my life to measure up to God's requirements?" Nothing could be more important.

It all begins in the mind. Then, what you put into your mind comes out in your words, and eventually what is in your words will come out in your actions. Good thoughts bear good fruit, and bad thoughts bear bad fruit, and you, the gardener, get to decide which you will have. You are the only one with the ability to chop out the weeds in your spirit and to plant good seeds. The seeds you need are found in the Word of God.

Examine carefully what you allow to take up residence in your mind. If you are having nightmares, bad dreams, and impure thoughts, it may be an indication that you are feeding your mind improperly. When impure thoughts come to you, they may simply be temptations from the enemy, or they may be the result of what you are feeding the mind. As the popular computer term states: trash in ... trash out. Nothing can come out of the mind that was not first allowed to enter it.

> *The devil has a way of taking advantage of everyone who is ignorant of his devices.*

We are all tempted with wrong thoughts, but there is a difference in being tempted and in entertaining a thought. Once you have allowed it to come in and to be entertained, many times it is then very difficult to get rid of it. This is the reason so many are becoming bound by pornography. They have allowed unclean thoughts into their minds and have entertained them, and now they can't get rid of them. This is dangerous because unclean thoughts lead to unclean actions, and wholesome thoughts lead to wholesome actions. This is why we are urged by the Scriptures:

Finally, brethren, whatsoever things are TRUE, whatsoever things are HONEST, whatsoever things are JUST, whatsoever things are PURE, whatsoever things are LOVELY, whatsoever

things are OF GOOD REPORT; if there be any VIRTUE, and
if there be any PRAISE, THINK ON THESE THINGS.

Philippians 4:8

True, honest, just, pure, lovely, good, virtuous thoughts lead us deeper into the presence of God. Unclean thoughts lead us father away from Him.

This is the reason that your spiritual enemy bombards your thoughts and tries to make it difficult for you to concentrate on truth. He doesn't want you meditating on the Word of God, because he surely doesn't want you entering more fully into the presence of God.

Ignorance Is Never Bliss

There is an old saying that "ignorance is bliss," but it's not true and never has been true. The enemy has a way of taking advantage of everyone who is ignorant of his devices. But he has been taking advantage of us long enough, and it's time to put an end to his victories. When we know God's Word and know that we can have whatever it says we can have, the enemy has no ground to stand on, and he leaves us alone.

Ignorance is one of Satan's most effective devices, and he loves it when we don't know what is rightfully ours. One prime example is the way he torments us about our past sins. He works hard to get our focus on past mistakes rather than on the glorious future God has prepared for each of us.

The enemy whispers, "You 'messed up,' and now you will never do anything for God again because everybody knows your mess. You might as well forget it."

But the Bible teaches something altogether different. It says that when a person has fallen, we should get them back up on their feet, restore them, and act as if nothing had ever happened. That's

God's attitude about our past. Your spiritual enemy is a liar, and we should reject his lies about our future.

Another area where Satan takes advantage of our ignorance is concerning our failures in ministry. Some people are discouraged by the smallest thing. They prepare a teaching and no one comes to hear them. They try to sing a special song, and they end up hitting every note on the keyboard but the right one. This experience seems so terrible to them, and they are so embarrassed by it, that they vow never to attempt anything for God again.

This is so foolish. So you failed; we all have. Get up, dust yourself off, and try again. You'll get it right.

God's not nearly as upset about your failure as you are. Imagine giving up on our children because they couldn't walk right the first time they tried. When they take a few steps and fall, do we cast them aside? Certainly not! We catch them, put them on their feet again and say, "Come on. You can do it." And they do. Would God, our loving heavenly Father, do any less for us?

Feelings vs. the Word of God

What does the Word of God say about our salvation? How do we know we are saved? The answers are found in God's Word. So, when the devil says, "You're not saved," you can answer, "Yes I am because Romans 10:13 says that if I confess with my mouth and believe in my heart , I *shall* be saved, and I have done that, so I *am* saved."

When you know and have a full assurance of salvation, your feelings cannot change the facts. And, when you know that salvation includes your healing, feeling bad physically cannot change the fact that you know you are healed. At times, you may not *feel* saved, but you know that you *are* saved because you know what the Word of God says, and nothing can change that fact. In the same way, at times you may not *feel* healed, but you know you *are* healed because you know what the Word of God says, and nothing can change that fact.

We need to make a declaration, but that declaration cannot be based on our own ideas. We also cannot just repeat something we have memorized. We must know what we are talking about, or the devil will knock us down every time.

This is why it would be good for you to memorize the scripture passages on your copy of My Decree (the last page of the book) because then you will know what the Word says about each of your benefits as a child of God. You can then make your confession daily, having the Word of God hidden in your heart. It is important that you do this, and not base your confession on my word, your pastor's word, or the word of some other brother or sister in Christ. The devil can overrun my word, your pastor's word, or the word of some one else, but he can never overrun the Word of God.

Having a knowledge of the truths of God can keep you in tough times. This is important because the Bible shows that we overcome by the word of our testimony:

> *And they overcame him by the blood of the Lamb, and by THE WORD OF THEIR TESTIMONY; and they loved not their lives unto the death.* Revelation 12:11

And, because we must stand on the Word, our testimonies must be one with the Word. We cannot say one thing and believe another. Study the Word of God until you know what your rights are, and then stand by your confession through the good and the bad.

Jesus has told us what to do when we are sick, or when others are sick:

They shall lay hands on the sick, and they shall recover.

Mark 16:18

If we know His promise and then act on it, we can expect Him to do His part.

Your Knowledge of Who You Are Gives You Authority

When my granddaughter Laci was three years old, there was a group of children playing on the church platform one day after service. She jumped up on the platform and yelled, "Okay, everybody off!"

Startled, all of the other little children stopped and looked at her.

"I said everybody off the platform," she demanded, and she made them all get off.

Later she came to me and said, "Mom, I made all those kids get off the platform."

"You did?" I said.

"Yeah," she answered. "I told them I was the in-charge kid. I told those kids that my grandpa is the pastor of the church, so that makes me the in-charge kid!"

I had to laugh. Laci knew who she was, and she knew that whatever she said was law among those children.

What about you? Are you aware of the authority you have in God? Are you using it effectively? Or is the devil still pushing you around?

Taming the Tongue Is Accomplished Only Through the Word of God

We know that it is important to allow God to tame our tongues, but how is that accomplished? The Bible says that we must hide God's Word in our hearts so that we will not sin against Him:

> *Thy word have I hid in mine heart, that I might not sin against thee.*   Psalm 119:11

When we don't know what the Word of God says, it is normal to say things that don't line up with His way of thinking. This is deadly because His words are *"life"* and *"health"* to our bodies:

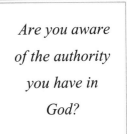

Are you aware of the authority you have in God?

> *My son, attend to my words; incline thine ear unto my sayings. Let them not depart from thine eyes; keep them in the midst of thine heart. For they are LIFE unto those that find them, and HEALTH to all their flesh.*   Proverbs 4:20-22

This word *health* meant medicine in the original Hebrew text.

Hiding the Word in our hearts also enables us to better guard against things that would damage us. This is important because out of our hearts flow *"the issues of life"*:

> *Keep thy heart with all diligence; for out of it are the issues of life.*   Proverbs 4:23

Everything in your life depends on what you think, and this is because what you think is what you say, and what you say is what you get.

Knowing this, David sang:

Let THE WORDS OF MY MOUTH, and THE MEDITATION

OF MY HEART, be acceptable in thy sight, O Lord, my strength, and my redeemer.   Psalm 19:14

What do you think about and meditate on from the time you get up in the morning until you go to bed at night? It matters. What is on your mind will be reflected in what comes out of your mouth during the course of the day, and that will determine the success or failure of your life.

Learning God's Will for Our Lives Changes Our Prayers

We often pray foolish prayers because our thinking is not right, and we haven't ascertained the will of God for our lives. For instance, a single woman might spot a sharply dressed, smooth-talking man, and begin to pray for him to be her husband. This is so foolish because this woman has no idea what might be on the inside of that man. He may look good, but looks sure aren't everything, and worse, they can be very deceiving.

God knows when what we want is for a carnal purpose. He said:

Ye ask, and receive not, because ye ask amiss, that ye may consume it upon your lusts.   James 4:3

Does God want you to get married and have a family? Or does He want you to concentrate on becoming a preacher of His Word?

Does He want you to work for a major corporation and earn well? Or does He want you to do volunteer work in ministry?

Every one of us needs to cry out to God: "Oh, God, what do YOU want me to do? What is YOUR purpose for my life?" Our own will is not the important thing, but *His* will for us. What He wants is always best for us. Our loving heavenly Father always knows best.

The Necessary Right Thinking

Some people have big plans that they express in prayer:

God, I would like to go to college and have a career. I'd like to climb the corporate ladder, and then, at thirty-five or forty, I would like to have a few children to raise. Then I'd like to sit back and enjoy a long retirement.

It's a well-thought-out plan, but is it God's will? It just might be God's will for you to serve as a missionary to Africa. If there are people in Africa waiting to hear the Gospel, and God has created you for the express purpose of preaching to them, would you ever be fulfilled climbing the corporate ladder? No, you would want to kill yourself before you ever reached the top. Your will must line up with God's will if you are to become effective in prayer.

Learn to pray unselfishly: "God, it's not what I want; it's what You want." This is one of the reasons it is so important to pray in the Spirit. After we have prayed our desires, we should say, "Now God, I've prayed my desire, but if this is not what You want for my life, I'm going to let the Holy Ghost take over and cancel out everything I prayed that is not Your will." The Holy Ghost knows the will of the Father for every saint, and He will be faithful to guide you.

A Positive Confession Based on Sound Thinking Leads to Unusual Miracles

One of our ministers was leading corporate prayer at the church, and he was praying God's will over the orphanage the church was attempting to establish in Brazil. He said, "Lord, I thank You that everything we need is already built in Brazil. Show it to us. Lead us to it, Lord. We believe and confess that the orphanage is already there."

When the staff member who was called to serve in the orphanage made a trip to Brazil, he called me from Sao Paulo to say that he had found a group of sixty-one orphans who were living in a facility condemned by the local government for abuses. If something didn't happen that week, these children would be sent back to the streets.

"Can you find someplace to house them?" I asked.

"I think I can," he assured me.

He located two large houses for rent, and within a month, we had sixty-one orphans under our care.

Since then, six more have been added. One of these was a boy who had slept on the street outside a shop. When he didn't move as fast as the shop owner wanted, he doused the boy with gasoline and set him on fire. The child suffered third-degree burns over two thirds of his body. A call from the hospital alerted our people, and he was taken in.

Truth makes us free only when we embrace it and become truth ourselves.

There are many more of these children of the streets in Brazil whom no one cares for, and I am believing God to give us the largest orphanage in all Sao Paulo. It is amazing what a simple word of faith based on the knowledge of God's Word can do!

When we first voiced our desire to have an orphanage in Brazil, local officials estimated that it would take us several years to put all of the necessary paperwork together to be able to get started. God knew how to shorten that time considerably. If He is for us, who can be against us? The world had better get out of our way.

We at Solid Rock Church spoke this miracle into existence based on our knowledge of the goodness of God. We could have said, "It looks like it will take us several years to get started, and surely we'll have to build some suitable facility. Maybe it's not God's will that we get started sooner. There seems to be too much opposition." But we didn't say that, and we got what we spoke.

Truth Makes You Free

Jesus taught very forcefully:

> *If ye continue in my word, then are ye my disciples indeed; and ye shall know the truth, and THE TRUTH SHALL MAKE YOU FREE.*   John 8:31-32

Some mistakenly quote this and say that the truth *sets* you free. It isn't the truth itself that sets us free. The truth is there the whole time, and yet an atheist may know it and still remain bound. Truth makes us free only when we embrace it and become truth ourselves.

When you know and understand the goodness of God, your thinking is right and you can begin to talk right and act right. And, before you know it, you are ready to pray with power and authority the prayer of faith.

Chapter 5

THE NECESSARY REWINDING
AND STARTING OVER

FOR BY THY WORDS thou shalt be justified, and by thy words thou shalt be condemned. Matthew 12:37

The prayer of faith is a prayer cleansed of negative confession. That's why we sometimes need to stop, rewind, and start all over again.

All of us have said things we should not have said, and our tongues get us into a world of trouble. But the more you realize how important your words are and that they can actually shape your future, the more you should want to just stop sometimes, recognize that what you have said is negative and carnal, not at all what God would say, and then tell yourself: "Wait a minute! Rewind and say that over again!" This time, say it in a way that is pleasing to God and the way that will bring you blessing.

You can even use this technique on others, but if you do, please do it with love. When you are talking to someone who is making a negative confession, look at them and say, "Wait a minute. Rewind that. Rephrase what you just said, and say it the way God would say it." Explain to them, if necessary, that what they say is what they will have. Throughout the ages people have spoken their destinies, and they are still doing it.

Two Opposing Confessions

In reality, most of us have two confessions—one of life and one of death. Ask a Christian in pain how they feel, and the answer may surprise you. With one breath, the person will say, "By His stripes I am healed," but with the very next breath, they will say, "I can't lie. I have been diagnosed with this illness, you know, and I can't deny that I have it." This second confession nullifies, or uproots, the first one, and the result is a contradiction.

On the one hand, the person is saying that they are healed, redeemed, and made whole, but at the same time, they are saying that the healing, redemption, and/or wholeness is not yet a fact in their body.

This person may believe that Christ can heal, but their confession is that Christ's healing power does not work for them. They have accepted a doctor's diagnosis and, therefore, do not realize what is theirs legally in Christ. The healing is there, but they have not accepted it.

When a person accepts the witness of physical evidence over the witness of the Word of God, they nullify the effect the Word could have in their life. Every time you confess a disease, a weakness, or a failure, you magnify your spiritual enemy above the Word of God, and you further destroy your confidence in His Word.

Confessing What You Cannot Yet See

Confessing that you do not have what you are actually experiencing or what you have been diagnosed with is not lying, as many have come to believe. The reason is that you are confessing what already is, meaning what has already been provided. It just hasn't been seen yet. Like Abraham before you, you are declaring what is not as though it were.

Abraham was told to take his son Isaac and to sacrifice him on a mountain in the land of Moriah. But Abraham's faith was such that just before he left he told his servant that he *and* Isaac would return (see Genesis 22:5).

How was that possible? Abraham knew that Isaac was the son of promise, the son from whom a new and holy nation would be born, and he therefore, knew that God would somehow work a miracle for him. Because of his confession (that he and Isaac would return), as he walked up one side of the mountain, God sent a ram to the other side of the mountain to take Isaac's place.

> *The ram had already been provided, even though Abraham could not yet see it.*

After their sacrifice was complete, Abraham *and* Isaac returned—just as Abraham had said. Did Abraham lie? No, the ram had already been provided, even though Abraham could not yet see it. He didn't need to see it. All he needed to do was believe God could provide it and confess that provision. And God did the rest.

The great battle, then, is to gain mastery over our confession, to learn that we can only have one confession at all times—not two opposing confessions, one positive and the other filled with negativity. It's not difficult to make your decree on a sunny day, but when the storm rages, and adverse circumstances hit, it is often a very different thing. When the enemy is trying to take advantage of you, can you still make your decree? Can you still say, "I am saved, I am healed, I am delivered, I am protected, I am preserved, I am made whole in the name of Jesus?" And can you do so without mentioning negative circumstances that might indicate otherwise?

YOUR LIFE FOLLOWS YOUR WORDS

The Testimony of Tom Brooks

God will use you greatly when you watch the words you sow and speak what you desire, avoiding negativity. This was amply proven by the testimony of Tom Brooks.

Tom was an illiterate from the hills of Kentucky. When he accepted Christ in the 1940s, he desired to read the Bible so that he could learn more about the Christian walk. One day he told his mother, "I'm going to the woods, and I'm not coming out until I can read the Word of God."

While Tom sat in the woods by a campfire he had kindled to warm himself, he quoted the only scripture verse he knew:

> ***For with God all things are possible.***   Mark 10:27

For the next several days, as he sat by his campfire praying, he periodically held up his Bible and declared:

> *For with God all things are possible!*
> *For with God all things are possible!*
> *For with God all things are possible!*

Seven days passed, and Tom Brooks still could not read. Still he continued to exclaim:

> *For with God all things are possible!*
> *For with God all things are possible!*
> *For with God all things are possible!*

He continued to vow never to come out of the woods until he had learned to read his Bible.

Very early on the eighth day, in the wee hours of the morning, Tom did just as he had before. He held up his Bible and declared:

The Necessary Rewinding and Starting Over

For with God all things are possible!
For with God all things are possible!
For with God all things are possible!

After again making this declaration, he decided to open his Bible, and when he did, his eyes landed on a page of the book of Psalm. Focusing on the first verse he saw, he began to read:

The Lord is my shepherd; I shall not want.   Psalm 23:1

Tom Brooks had miraculously read a verse from the Bible. He was so excited that he read another verse, and then another and another until finally he could stand it no longer. He jumped up and ran out of the woods and through the nearby hollows shouting, "God taught me to read! God taught me to read!"

It was so early that everyone was still sleeping, and normally Tom would have respected that, but this time he could not hold his excitement. "Get up! Get up!" he shouted. "God taught me how to read!"

Tom Brooks went on to make history because of his positive faith. He became a professor of theology at Berea College—although he was never able to read anything else but the Bible. This simple man from the hills of Kentucky could have dwelt on the negatives in his life, but he refused to, and God honored him because of it.

Faith and Confession Freed from Doubt Moves Mountains

A friend of ours who actually knew Tom Brooks told us a very interesting story about him. His simple faith and declaration literally moved a mountain.

YOUR LIFE FOLLOWS YOUR WORDS

Tom's father, upon his death, left his son a piece of land in the country across the road from their home. The land was located on the side of a mountain, a mountain so steep that it was said that even a billy goat could not climb to the top of it.

Tom came home one day and told his mother, "Mamma, God told me to build a church."

"Where are you going to build it, Tom?" she asked.

"Across the road," he answered with confidence.

> *God will move heaven and earth for you when you stand on His Word and are careful to avoid negativity in your confession.*

Puzzled, she replied, "Tom, have you looked at that mountain lately? It's much too steep. How are you going to build a church on that mountain?"

He said, "Well, the Word of God said that if I speak to my mountain and command it to be removed, God would move it."

She was surprised at his literal interpretation of that verse and assured him that it was *not* to be taken so literally. "What Jesus meant by that teaching," she explained, "was that if there's something in your life too big for you to handle, He would move it out of the way if you continued to confess it."

"But that's not what the Bible says," Tom protested. "It says that if I speak to my mountain and command it to be removed, God will move it. So I'm going back to the woods, and I'm not coming out until God moves that mountain across the road."

Tom's mother could not believe what she was hearing. She ran and told her preacher and some of her friends what was happening with Tom and asked them to pray.

Many days passed, and Mrs. Brooks was constantly thinking of her son and how she could help him. Surely he was in for a disappointment. How could he expect God to move his mountain?

One day there came a knock at the door of the Brooks' residence. Mrs. Brooks answered the door, and there stood a strange man. He asked her who owned the mountain across the road. Mrs. Brooks said her son owned it. The man asked if he could speak with him. "He's in the woods somewhere, and I don't know how to reach him," she answered.

"We've been strip mining behind that mountain for a couple of years now," the man told her, and we're looking for soil to fill the trenches we have dug. If he'll allow us to buy the dirt from that mountain, we'll push it off into those strip mines."

"Wait here!" Mrs. Brooks said, and she ran into the woods, shouting to her son as she ran, "Tom, come home, Honey! God just moved your mountain!"

God Will Fulfill a
Confession Void of Negativity

God will move heaven and earth for you when you stand on His Word and are careful to avoid negativity in your confession. He watches over His Word that you speak in faith to perform it for you:

I will hasten my word TO PERFORM IT.   Jeremiah 1:12

As we began the year 2003 at Solid Rock Church, we knew that we would see more unusual and undeniable miracles that we had seen during the past ten years combined. The reason was that we had decreed it to be so. With our new-found knowledge and accompanying power, all we had to do was decree a thing, and God would begin to work to bring it to pass, if necessary bringing dead things back to life.

Before I began to preach one Sunday, I said, "Somebody is going to get saved today. I don't know who you are, but you are here, and you will be saved before you leave this place." I expected and decreed the miracle of salvation to take place in the service, and, sure enough, several were saved that day. The exact opposite is happening in churches around the globe because the exact opposite confession is being made.

One pastor said to my husband, "People are not getting saved at our church anymore."

"Tell me," Lawrence said, "you don't expect someone to get saved in every service, do you?"

"Well, no," the pastor answered.

"Then that's why no one is getting saved," Lawrence said.

That pastor had sowed with his negative words the empty harvest he was reaping at the altar.

Put Your Mouth On a Fast

There are several things we can do to train ourselves not to speak negativity. One of them that I have found to be helpful is to put your mouth on a fast. This will not be a fast from food, as we normally understand a fast, but a fast from speaking negativity. During this period of fasting, be very conscious of every word you say, remembering that every one of them is forming your world. Speak the truth of God at all times because it is *"the truth"* (the truth of God concerning you) that *"shall make you free"* (John 8:32).

What if I said to you, "For the next three days, everything that comes out of your mouth will happen"? What would your confession be? I'm sure that it would change a great deal.

You may think that the likelihood that everything that comes out of your mouth happening is a remote one, but according to the Word of God, everything you say and believe *will* happen. So this is serious. If you can speak the truth of God, you will be free. But if you speak the lies of the enemy, you will be bound. This is a basic principle of life, and yet many people live out their entire lives without ever once considering the impact their words have made on their world. Your life follows your words.

Your life follows your words.

If this describes you, put yourself on a word fast, abstaining from the lies of Satan, and watch your world blossom before your very eyes and become what God destined it to be. You will never regret doing this.

Retraining Your Tongue

Be advised that it will take discipline to train your mouth to say what God says about you. Most of us have been trained to speak everything else *but* the Word of God. Most of us speak the negative things our parents said about us, the negative things a doctor has said, or the negative things friends may have told us. Rarely do we speak what God tells us in His Word.

If you are keeping company with people who speak negative things into your life, now is the time to get away from them. If you don't, you will soon begin to believe what they say about you. Then it won't be long before you begin to say about yourself what they are saying about you. And those negative things will become your new reality.

When you catch yourself saying negative things about yourself, or anyone else for that matter, say to yourself, "Uh oh! Watch what you say! Back up! Rewind!"

Then, rewind what you just said and say it over. This time, say

YOUR LIFE FOLLOWS YOUR WORDS

what God says about the situation. In this way, you can break the habit of listening to and speaking what others say about you. You must do this if you want to break out of the prison of negative confession. Such a confession has kept you in bondage year in and year out, but the right kind of confession will make your free.

If you're single and desire to be married, don't say: "I've been single for so many years now that it looks like I'll never find anyone to marry. Maybe God wants me to be single for the rest of my life. There will *never* be someone for me." God may indeed want you to be single for the rest of your life, but if He doesn't, don't let your negative confession rob you of the spouse He has prepared for you.

If you are single, use this time to be alone with yourself and with God. While you are waiting, get to know God and what He desires for you. Serve in some kind of ministry, and while you are serving, pray for the spouse God is sending your way.

Whatever you do, don't get anxious. You or your prospective spouse must need some "fixing up," or you would already be joined together. Ask God to use this intervening time to make you what He wants you to be for your spouse and to make your spouse what you need him or her to be.

As we have seen, when you speak you are sowing seeds that will surely germinate and bring forth fruit. Jesus taught about a sower who went out to sow (see Luke 8:4-15). The seed this sower sowed was the Word of God, and you must also choose good seed to sow if you expect a good harvest. No seed is better than what God has said.

Anytime you speak death, or hear someone else speaking death, yell, "Rewind!" Then make yourself or your friends turn the confession of death into a confession of life. Force yourself to sow words of life at all times, and help those around you to do the same.

What harvest are you reaping as a direct result of your sowing? If your results are unfavorable, there is hope. Rewind your decree. Start over, and this time say what God says about you. Decree something that is consistent with the truths of salvation: "I am saved, I am healed, I am delivered, I am protected, I am preserved, I am made whole in the name of Jesus," and watch God establish you in the path of your desire.

Reports of Victory

A lady called me to report a miracle she had received after retraining her speech because she had heard me preach this message. She said, "I had to have two thousand dollars, and I started confessing, 'God, You're going to meet my need. I don't know where it's coming from, but I've got to have two thousand dollars, and I know You're going to supply it.' " In this way, rather than confess defeat and lack, she confessed the bounty of the Lord and His love for her. A few days later, she received a check in the mail for four thousand dollars she hadn't realized was owed to her. She received what she needed because she asked in faith, praying her desire, and not her problem.

Once your talk begins to change, then your walk will also change. And you will be ready for a great destiny in God. If you allow God to retrain your tongue and tame it for a lifetime, there is no limit to the great things that might come of it.

It is time that we leave behind much of the baggage that has hindered our growth. There are wagons full of "junk" that we've been dragging around behind us for years. Get rid of it, and see what God will do. Your future is too bright for you to continue being hindered by the darkness of wrong confession. Come out of that into God's glorious tomorrows.

I received a letter from a young lady who was suffering two ailments: a herniated disk and a brain concussion. Both of these had caused her excruciating pain. She had confessed her healing, but she still had a lot of pain. She told me in the letter that the Lord revealed to her what her problem was. Just as she was about to receive her miracle, she would begin to murmur and complain about the pain she was experiencing. The Lord told her that she had no right to murmur or complain about her situation, and that if she confessed and believed she was healed, she *was* healed.

> *Once your talk begins to change, then your walk will also change.*

He also told her she had three options whenever she was having pain: she could confess "I am healed," she could pray in the Spirit, or she could simply keep silent. It worked. She was healed. Any of these three methods avoided the negativity of confessing her situation above the promise of the Word of God. And this brought her victory.

Learning to Ignore Intimidating Enemies

Sometimes it seems nearly impossible to ignore the big enemies that come up against us and to make a positive confession in the light of their presence. When the armies of Israel spoke doubt and unbelief concerning the giant Goliath (and that included David's own brothers), they were looking at what they saw through their natural eyes. The physical makeup of the man Goliath was indeed intimidating. Some say that he may have been as much as thirteen feet tall. Imagine it!

Saul and David served the same God. Still, Saul saw Goliath as being huge, and David saw Goliath as being small. Saul was looking with his own eyes, but David was looking through the eyes of the Lord. Because of this, David easily defeated Goliath. It was David's faith that propelled that rock and gave him the victory.

The Necessary Rewinding and Starting Over

Making our problems bigger than they really are is even a problem for those of us who pray for the sick. We are sometimes inclined to pray for the easy cases first. A headache seems so much easier to receive healing for than blindness, for example. Wheelchair patients or those who are obviously invalid are often shunted aside into special sections reserved for the "difficult" cases. But is anything too hard for God?

Jeremiah asked that question on God's behalf:

Behold, I am the Lord, the God of all flesh: is there anything too hard for me? Jeremiah 32:27

The understood answer is no; nothing is too hard for God. He is able to deal with every situation of life. So we have no reason to speak negativity—even when faced with imposing enemies.

When David saw Goliath and heard the foolish comments the military men were making about him, he didn't hesitate. He could have said, with justification, that he would wait until he was sixteen to enlist in the service of his nation. But, no, David didn't know any negative thinking. He boldly announced:

This day will the Lord deliver thee into mine hand. 1 Samuel 17:46

"This day." Imagine a boy speaking to a giant in that way. But it worked. Very soon David was taking Goliath's head off. He spoke the word, refusing to be intimidated by what he saw and to respond with negativity, and the giant of a man fell.

David was just a boy, but when he spoke what God had said, refusing to entertain any negative thoughts or words, God honored it. And that same tactic will work for you.

Learn to cleanse your thoughts and words of negativity, and you will soon be ready to pray with power the prayer of faith.

Chapter 6

THE NECESSARY PERSEVERANCE

Let us HOLD FAST the profession of our faith without wavering; (for he is faithful that promised). Hebrews 10:23

The prayer of faith is a prayer of perseverance.

It is one thing to have faith in God and to make a declaration of His promises to us, but it is quite another thing to hold on to that declaration in the face of our spiritual enemy's constant taunts. He will tell you that you are not yet what God wants you to be—and never will be.

It is one thing to confess God's promises when you are in the presence of other believers in a power-packed worship service, but it is quite another thing to hold on to that promise when you find yourself all alone on the battlefields of life. But faith that cannot persevere is faith that cannot have the final victory. Therefore you must learn not only to believe and to confess what you believe, but you must also learn to hold on to your belief and also to your confession of that belief.

"Hold Fast"

Each of us must learn to lay hold of everything that God has promised us and then not waver—no matter what our symptoms indicate, no matter how our financial statement reads. Otherwise, you will speak life one day to your situation and death the next. This is tempting and easy to do because circumstances change on a daily basis, just like the stock market does—up one day and down the next. Wavering in this way can be deadly when it relates to our faith and our confession of faith. The apostle James declared:

Let him ask in faith, NOTHING WAVERING. For HE THAT WAVERETH is like a wave of the sea driven with the wind and tossed. For let not that man think that he shall receive ANY THING of the Lord. A double minded man is unstable IN ALL HIS WAYS. James 1:6-8

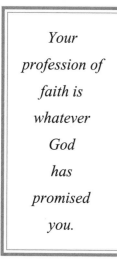

Your profession of faith is whatever God has promised you.

The man who wavers in his faith and in his confession of faith will receive nothing.

It was my perseverance that brought me out of poverty. I had to stand firm through my late teens and early twenties, as I drove that retired taxicab with the rusted-out floorboards. Even as I drove it about, I would confess, "It won't always be this way. One day I'll have the best car money can buy because I am the head and not the tail. I am the apple of my Father's eye. I am above and not beneath." I refused to allow the negative circumstances of life to rob me of my destiny, and I tenaciously clung to God's promises for me. Otherwise, they would never have materialized.

You must learn to keep your confession of faith in the face of every threat, every negative circumstance, and every trial that comes your way. The writer of the book of Hebrews said it this way:

Seeing that we have a great high priest, that is passed into the

heavens, Jesus the Son of God, let us HOLD FAST to our pro-
fession. Hebrews 4:14

Your *profession* of faith, or your covenant, promise, decree, or confession, is whatever God has promised you. By faith get a grip on it, and then don't let it go in the face of anything you might hear, anything you might see, or anything you might feel ... until what God has spoken becomes a reality.

Just because you don't see what you desire in the natural realm doesn't mean that it doesn't exist. Actually it *does* exist in the spiritual realm, because it *has* to first exist in the spiritual realm before it can ever manifest itself in the natural realm. Everything you desire must be released first in the spirit before it becomes a reality in your life. It's there; just believe for it and keep believing until you see it.

Laughing At Your Symptoms

It makes no difference what your symptoms say. Laugh at the symptoms and command the author of the illness to leave your body. I employ this principal every chance I get.

I went out on a really brisk day this past winter with nothing warm on my feet, just hose and slip-on shoes, and I felt the cold. (I have the habit of dressing the same wherever I go, with no real thought for the weather. And, for those who are not familiar with our Ohio winters, it can get very cold and damp outside.) Before I knew it, I began to feel my throat draw up, and that is always a sign to me that the enemy is trying to put something on me.

The next day I went to the mall to do some shopping, and I began to experience chills so bad that I told the people I was with that I needed to go home immediately. I could sense that something serious was coming on. (Anytime I want to leave a shopping mall early, something is really wrong with me, because I *love* to shop.) As soon as I got home, I went right to bed.

It was only after I was in bed that I suddenly came to my senses. I was accepting what the enemy was sending my way, and I couldn't afford to do that. I said, "In the name of Jesus, Satan you can't attack this body because I am saved, I am healed, I am delivered, I am protected, I am preserved, I am made whole," and I went off to sleep.

During the night, I woke up several times with cold symptoms, but each time I prayed, "God, I thank You that I am saved, I am healed, I am delivered, I am protected, I am preserved, and I am made whole in the name of Jesus."

The next morning Lawrence asked me how I felt, and I replied, "I feel wonderful because I'm saved!" But I was not just confessing what I was believing would come. I *was* feeling fine. That good outcome was due to my confession and my standing on that confession—even when I hadn't felt well physically. Our bodies have to line up with whatever our minds are communicating to them—if we persevere in the face of every negative symptom. Your life follows your words.

Speaking the Word in Your Need and Not Falling Into the Mouthtrap

Speak the Word in the face of your need. Say, "I don't know how God will get my house payment to me, but I know it's on its way. It's not my job to be concerned with how He will do it. My job is to pay my tithes and offerings, and I've done that. So Jehovah-Jireh, my Provider who took care of me yesterday and has promised to go with me into all my tomorrows, will provide for me everything I need today." And then hold fast to that confession.

Go around the house singing and dancing, making your own music and using your own words. You might want to start by singing: "Jehovah-Jireh, my Provider, His grace is sufficient for me," but then add your own words.

By doing this, you are saying, "I know that my situation looks hopeless, but that doesn't change God. He is my Provider, and He will make a way for me."

If you can go about dusting your house, singing your own song and dancing your own dance before the Lord in victory and in anticipation of what He has already provided for you, that is so much better and so much more productive than murmuring. Some say, "Oh, Lord, it looks like I'm going to have to go to the loan company and take out another loan on my house." When you do that, your spiritual enemy jumps for glee, and shouts, "We've got them! We've got them! They snared themselves with their own words! They fell into the mouth trap!"

Pressing Through

Satan will do everything he possibly can to sow confusion so that your confession of healing is blocked. One example is the tendency of the media to go after the men and women that God is using in the healing arena and to try to find something with which to smear their good names. They try to make all of the best-known and loved men and women of faith look bad. When someone they have prayed for dies, the media jumps on that, as if it were some personal failure on their part. Don't be caught up in this or any other confusion the enemy tries to propagate.

It is YOUR faith that determines your outcome. If your desire is spoken forth in faith, and you hold fast to it, I believe you will receive. Press through the confusion.

YOUR LIFE FOLLOWS YOUR WORDS

A woman in the Bible who had suffered for many years with an issue of blood said to herself:

> **If I may but touch his garment, I shall be whole.**
>
> Matthew 9:21

This *if* was not whether or not she could be healed. She considered her healing to be a given and said, *"I shall be whole."* The question was whether or not she had the strength to press through the crowd to touch Jesus and receive the healing that she knew was already hers. Could she persevere until it became reality?

Press through. The enemy is trying to put people and things in your way to keep you from receiving the miracle that is just waiting for you. People are telling you that you can't have your miracle, that it's just too hard for you to obtain, that you can't get to it. But if you can press through doubt, press through unbelief, and press past all those who are trying to hinder you, you can have it—and you *will* have it. Press through all public opinion and receive your miracle today.

The prophet Daniel had to press through another type of opposition. He went on a twenty-one-day fast because he needed some answers from God. While he was praying concerning his desire, he reminded God of His promises. He spoke out what he desired, and when he did that the devil began to throw opposition his way—just as he does with you and me.

The opposition against Daniel was serious, straight from the pits of hell, and it came in the form of an evil principality who attempted to prevent the answer to Daniel's prayer (which was even then being delivered from God by the angel Gabriel) from getting to the prophet. This opposition continued for twenty-one days, with a great battle raging in the heavens. Finally, God sent forth Michael, Gabriel's backup, and Michael held off the demon until Gabriel could get the needed answer through to Daniel.

It is interesting to see what Gabriel said to Daniel when he finally reached him:

> *Fear not, Daniel: for FROM THE FIRST DAY that thou didst set thine heart to understand, and to chasten thyself before thy God, THY WORDS WERE HEARD, and I am come FOR THY WORDS.*   Daniel 10:12

An angel had been dispatched to deliver Daniel's answer the very first day he spoke the words and reminded God of His promise. The enemy had tried to stop delivery of the answer, but he couldn't stop what God had already started—as long as Daniel stood firm. All Daniel had to do was hold fast to his confession and remain true, and the answer (that had been on the way all along) arrived.

It is YOUR faith that determines your outcome

Holding Fast Shows Your Continued Faith

When you confess God's Word, you are confirming that you have confidence in the God Who said it, and as you hold fast to that confession, it shows your continued trust—in the face of contradictory circumstances. The prophet Nahum noted:

> *The LORD is good, a strong hold in the day of trouble; and HE KNOWETH THEM THAT TRUST IN HIM.*   Nahum 1:7

He knows, and He has sent the answer on its way. So don't waver.

God knows when we trust Him initially, and He knows when we continue to trust Him. So hold fast your confession until you see the answer.

There are many good doctors, God heals through them, and it's okay if you need one. The problem for many is that doctors give us negative reports that hurt our faith. Whatever you do, don't give up on your healing. Hold fast to God's promise.

When the Lord healed a certain blind man in the Bible, He reached down and took some dirt, representing humanity, spit on it, put the mud on the man's eyes and then told him to go wash in the pool of Siloam (see John 9:1-12). Through this miracle, Jesus showed that some healings would come through medical intervention. But, however your healing comes, hold on until it gets to you.

Some become discouraraged when their healing does not come in the way someone else's has. Many call me and ask me to tell them exactly how I was healed so that they can expect the same thing, but God may not bring your healing in that same way. Each person needs to respond on their own level of faith, and each one needs to hold on to their confession until victory comes.

If you are faced with a serious sickness, know that it is an attack from hell. Therefore, you must stand and fight with your faith and your confession of the Word—even when adverse circumstances seem to prevail.

God says that when we have done all we can do, then we just need to stand:

> *Wherefore take unto you the whole armour of God, that ye may be able to withstand in the evil day, and having done all, to stand.*
> Ephesians 6:13

The Necessary Perseverance

If you can stand and not *"grow weary in well doing,"* confessing the promises of the Word of God, you will reap, but only if we *"faint not"*:

> **And let us not be weary in well doing: for in due season we shall reap, if we faint not.**   Galatians 6:9

What we often do is to confess that we are healed when the symptoms of the sickness have subsided, but as soon as we begin to get some serious pain, we lose our confession and say instead, "I thought I was healed." That statement pulls your confession of health out by the roots, and you will get nothing from God if you live your life in this way.

"Faint not!" Regardless of what comes your way, you must stand and say, "The seed is planted, and if I water it by decreeing and believing in my heart, it will produce a fruit that will bring forth my miracle." That fruit will come as you stand on the Word of God.

Strengthening Your Ability to Persevere

What can you do to have greater perseverance in your faith and confession?

For one, don't let this teaching get away from you. Read this book over and over until it's message is firmly implanted into your heart. Get some of my tapes on this subject and listen to them again and again. Take "My Decree" out and study it. Meditate on the corresponding scriptures until this word gets into your spirit. Even after you feel that you have captured it, review it once in a while. If you fail to keep it before you, you may slip right back into your old habit of speaking negative words, and thus cursing yourself and others. And whatever comes your way, continue to hold on to your knowledge of what Jesus has done for you.

Every single day, make your confession that you are saved, healed, delivered, protected, preserved, and made whole in the name of Jesus, and that you intend to walk in this confession whatever comes. After months of doing that, you will be surprised to find that you are no longer among the feeble.

> *You are basing your confession upon the promise of the unfailing Word of God.*

Resist wrong thoughts. Sometimes the enemy tries to put wrong thoughts in my mind, but I simply refuse to entertain them. "Are you really saved?" he asks. "After all, that thought you just had was not very Christ-like."

Knowing that the thought isn't mine, I refuse to accept it. Then I begin to confess that I have the mind of Christ, and I make sure that my helmet of salvation is secure so that it can repel the fiery darts of the enemy that are trying to penetrate my mind (see Ephesians 6:17).

We Are Much Too Quick to Waver

In all of my years of serving God, I have never once questioned my salvation. It hasn't mattered that I was not perfect. The fact of being tempted to think some bad thought or of actually saying something unkind to or about someone out of frustration has never caused me to doubt that I knew the Lord and that He was my Savior. And a great majority of Christians would agree with me on this point. Then, why is it so easy for Satan to make us doubt our healing? Let a little pain come along, and we are much too quick to listen to his taunts:

> *You just thought you were healed.*
> *You told others that you were healed, but you still have that lump.*

108

The Necessary Perseverance

You said you were healed, but you still have that recurring pain in your stomach.

The devil is a liar, so it doesn't really matter if you still have a lump or some pain. If you say you are healed and you hold fast to that confession, then you *are* healed. If the Word of God says it, then *you* can say it too. Remember, your life follows your words.

You are not saying you are healed because Darlene Bishop said it; you are basing your confession upon the promise of the unfailing Word of God. And because the Word of God never changes, your confession should not change—whatever comes your way.

It's Easy When Everything Is Going Well

Always remember, as you believe and confess and prepare to reap your corresponding harvest, the thief of the seed, Satan, will try to steal your harvest before it becomes a reality. Make your decree that you are saved, healed, delivered, protected from the devourer of your harvest, preserved, and made whole in the name of Jesus, and then stand by that confession so that you can enjoy the treasure laid up for you by our great God. Expect opposition, but expect to hold fast through that opposition:

> *The thief does not come except to steal, and to kill, and to destroy. I have come that they may have life, and that they might have it more abundantly.*　　　　　　　　John 10:10

Anytime God decides to do a great work, the enemy is there to try to block it. Whenever any great harvest is about to be reaped, your spiritual enemy always comes to try to steal that harvest. He is on a mission to *"steal, kill, and destroy,"* and he will use any means necessary to accomplish his ends. Recognize his methods, and defeat him through perseverance in faith.

Everyone can say, "I am healed," when there is no pain, no lumps, and no bumps. But what about when pain is wracking your body, and you find a lump or a bump? Can you still say, "It doesn't matter what comes and what goes; let the winds blow and the storms rage, I am still healed; I praise you Jesus, for You are my Healer"?

Hold fast to your confession—even in the face of apparent defeat. You may have received divorce papers in the mail, for example, but don't be moved by that. This is just the enemy, and you don't have to accept his lies into your marriage. Confess, "My marriage is whole. My man [or woman] doesn't know it, but he [or she] is coming back." And stand on that confession until it becomes reality.

Whatever your particular situation is, whatever your attack from the evil one, whatever the crisis you happen to be facing today, know that you will be victorious as you persevere in faith and hold fast your confession to the glory of God.

If you can learn this secret of holding fast to your confession of faith in the face of every adversity, you are ready to pray with power and effectiveness the prayer of faith.

Chapter 7

The Necessary Passion

The effectual FERVENT prayer of a righteous man availeth much.   James 5:16

Praying always with all prayer and SUPPLICATION in the Spirit, and watching thereunto with all perseverance and SUPPLICATION for all saints.   Ephesians 6:18

The prayer of faith is a prayer of passion, a prayer of *"supplication"*:

What Is Supplication?

Supplication is more than simple petitioning or reading off a list of our requests in prayer. The person praying this type of prayer experiences an intensity, a passion, in what they are saying and in why they are saying it. This type of prayer—the passionate, fervent, supplicatory prayer—results from a deep desire on their part, and the result is that they pour out their hearts at the feet of Jesus. Such a prayer always moves the heart of God.

Dictionary.com gives the meaning of *supplicate* as: "(1) To ask for humbly or earnestly, as by praying. (2) To make a humble entreaty to; beseech." It goes on to show that in its common use, supplication comes very close to begging.

The King James Bible agrees heartily with this interpretation, for the root word translated *"effectual fervent prayer"* in the King James actually means red hot prayer (James 5:16). That is about as passionate as one can get. But why get so worked up for people who sometimes hardly seem to care about themselves and have often given up on life? Because God loves them passionately, and when we feel His heartbeat, we will love them too.

It's time to get serious with God in prayer. We are clearly living in the last days, and we no longer have time to act like children playing church. Millions are dying and going to hell, and someone needs to become bothered enough by that fact to passionately go before the Lord and intercede for them before it's too late. If you don't care, who will?

If we don't care if people live or die, then our prayers will reflect that fact. If we don't care who suffers from sickness and pain, then what can we expect from our prayers for the sick? It is the serious prayers—passionate prayers, fervent prayers, red hot prayers—that touch the heart of God and bring the desired results.

When delivering his teaching on the prayer of faith to the early Church, James not only included this phrase *"effectual fervent prayer,"* but he also included this amazing statement relating to it:

> ***Elias was a man subject to like passions as we are, and he prayed earnestly that it might not rain: and it rained not on the earth by the space of three years and six months. And he prayed again, and the heaven gave rain, and the earth brought forth her fruit.***   James 5:17-18

Elias (or Elijah) was a man just like us, but his prayer was so fervent that it caused the natural rains to cease for forty-two months, and then his faith-filled, red-hot prayer caused it to rain again. You, too, can start doing the impossible when your prayer reflects a genuine concern for God's will.

Nehemiah's Passionate Concern for Jerusalem

When Nehemiah, who was living in exile in Babylon, learned that his beloved city Jerusalem was in ruins, he wept for days on end before God:

> *And it came to pass, when I heard these words, that I sat down and wept, and mourned certain days, and fasted, and prayed before the God of heaven.*   Nehemiah 1:4

Others of the exiles may have been praying prayers for Jerusalem too, but Nehemiah *"wept," "mourned," "fasted,"* and *"prayed."* Because of this, it was *his* prayer that touched the heart of God.

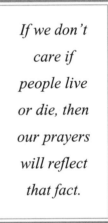

If we don't care if people live or die, then our prayers will reflect that fact.

Why did Nehemiah even care? He was doing well in Babylon, having worked his way up to the very trusted position of cupbearer to the heathen king. Why not leave well enough alone? What did Jerusalem have to do anymore with his life in Babylon? Most of the other exiles didn't care, so why should he?

But that was the very thing that set Nehemiah apart and made his prayers effective. He *did* care. He cared passionately, so passionately that he could not hide his concern, as he took it to God *"day and night"*:

> *Let thine ear now be attentive, and thine eyes open, that thou mayest hear the prayer of thy servant, which I pray before thee now, DAY AND NIGHT, for the children of Israel thy servants.*   Nehemiah 1:6

It was clear from Nehemiah's prayer that evil had come upon the city of Jerusalem because of the sins of her people. So, if they had sinned, they were receiving just what they deserved, were they not? Why should Nehemiah be bothered about them?

But someone had to carry this burden. Someone had to feel the heartbeat of God. Someone had to know His mind and pray it forth so that it could become reality. Since Nehemiah was the one willing to do that, God chose him. And Nehemiah, moved with passion for the needs of his people and his city, prayed fervently before God *"day and night"* about the matter.

It wasn't long before the king became aware of Nehemiah's unexplainable obsession with a far-off city and a sinful and scattered people:

> *It came to pass in the month Nisan, in the twentieth year of Artaxerxes the king, that wine was before him: and I took up the wine, and gave it unto the king. Now I had not been beforetime sad in his presence. Wherefore the king said unto me, Why is thy countenance sad, seeing thou art not sick? this is nothing else but sorrow of heart. Then I was very sore afraid.*
>
> Nehemiah 2:1-2

Nehemiah had every right to be afraid. His obsession had now placed his work in jeopardy and possibly even his very life. Often those who displeased a heathen king were executed without delay or remedy. Nehemiah knew all of this, but he still could not hide his genuine concern for his people and for the holy city Jerusalem.

Why Bother?

It is all too true in our modern world that many people seem to be able to go about the daily routine of their lives caring not one thing for those who are less fortunate than they—those who have not heard the Gospel, those who have gone astray and are suffering the consequences of their folly, those who constitute "the unfortunates" of this world. Relatively few people care about the homeless or why and how they got that way, about our addicts and alcoholics, about our nearly two million prisoners shut away out of our sight. Because we can't see them, it becomes easy to put them out of our minds and hearts as well.

But God has not forgotten the orphans (fatherless), the homeless, the strangers (foreigners), the widows and the imprisoned of this world. He, in fact, has declared Himself their friend and benefactor:

> *A father of the fatherless, and a judge of the widows,* **is God in** *his holy habitation.*   Psalm 68:5

> *The* LORD *preserveth the strangers; he relieveth the fatherless and widow.*   Psalm 146:9

We are commanded by God to remember those who are imprisoned just as if we were there imprisoned with them:

> *Remember them that are in bonds, as bound with them;* **and** *them which suffer adversity, as being yourselves also in the body.*   Hebrews 13:3

While He was on earth, Jesus was criticized for being *"a friend of publicans and sinners"* (Matthew 11:19). He loved sinners so much that He wept for them. He even wept for Jerusalem, where He was often rejected and ridiculed and where He was eventually executed:

> *And when he was come near, he beheld the city, and WEPT OVER IT.*   Luke 19:41

115

YOUR LIFE FOLLOWS YOUR WORDS

O Jerusalem, Jerusalem, which killest the prophets, and stonest them that are sent unto thee; how often would I have gathered thy children together, as a hen doth gather her brood under her wings, and ye would not!   Luke 13:34

Such a passionate concern for fallen man must seem very strange to most people, even ridiculous, but it is wholly explained by God's love for His creation. He said:

For God so loved the world, that he gave his only begotten Son, that whosoever believeth in him should not perish, but have everlasting life.   John 3:16

> *If we have accepted God's mercy and love, how can we not then give mercy and love to a dying world around us?*

Those of this world rejected Jesus and hated Him so much they wanted to kill Him, and eventually they did, but still Jesus loved them and willingly gave Himself for them. He was passionate about what He did, so we, as the inheritors of His message and ministry, must be passionate about what we do as well. And since God has the answers the world needs, and we communicate with Him through prayer, He requires that our prayers be passionate and fervent.

God loves the weak, and the poor, and so should we. The prophet Joel declared:

Let THE WEAK say, I am strong.   Joel 3:10

God does not despise *"the weak,"* like so many of us do these days. He does not despise *"the poor,"* as is common in our affluent society:

He raiseth up THE POOR out of the dust, and lifteth up the beggar from the dunghill, to set them among princes, and to make them inherit the throne of glory: for the pillars of the earth are the LORD's, and he hath set the world upon them.

1 Samuel 2:8

If we have accepted God's mercy and love, how can we not then give mercy and love to a dying world around us?

Jesus Felt Compassion for the Suffering

Jesus healed and otherwise blessed people because He was moved by their suffering. He felt genuine compassion for them:

But when he saw the multitudes, HE WAS MOVED WITH COMPASSION on them, because they fainted, and were scattered abroad, as sheep having no shepherd.   Matthew 9:36

And Jesus went forth, and saw a great multitude, and WAS MOVED WITH COMPASSION toward them, and he healed their sick.   Matthew 14:14

Then Jesus called his disciples unto him, and said, I HAVE COMPASSION ON THE MULTITUDE, because they continue with me now three days, and have nothing to eat: and I will not send them away fasting, lest they faint in the way.

Matthew 15:32

The type of compassion, or passion, that Jesus felt for people in need is rather rare in our modern world. But the tragedy is that somehow even we Christians have adopted the attitudes of those around us.

They made their bed; now let them sleep in it.
I guess now they will learn their lesson.
What did they expect? They're just paying the piper.
How do you suppose people get themselves into such messes?

It has almost gotten to the point that we think if we help some-one we're doing them a disservice. They have to learn that there are consequences to their actions, so we should just let them rot in their filth until they wake up and decide to pull themselves up by their own bootstraps. If we give anything to those in need, it is con-sidered by many that we are jeopardizing their ability to learn to stand on their own two feet. Rather than give them a fish, the mod-ern axiom goes, we should teach them to fish.

But we certainly didn't get *any* of these concepts from the Bible, God's Holy Word. There we find love and compassion and an out-stretched hand to those who are fallen. God delights in lifting up the fallen, restoring the broken, and using those considered unus-able. Until we can begin to feel His heartbeat and know and understand His thoughts for the needy, we will never pray effective prayers for them.

Compassionate Confession

Some people will go to hell, some of them our own children, because we have put them there with our unloving and judgmen-tal mouths. We have said things to them like:

He'll never make it; he'll backslide within a week.
He is so sorry, lowdown, and lost that he'll never find his way
back to God.
My child is such a brat.

The Necessary Passion

You heathen. Why do you act this way?
Child, you are the worst liar I have ever met in my life.

What spirit is it that compels us to say such things? When we do this, we speak death to the very people we are called to love and rescue. Tell those around you who they are in Christ and what they can do and be in Him. Stop cursing your own children.

I always think of what happened to Gideon of the Old Testament. He lived during a time of particularly bad oppression, and when the biblical scene opens on him, we find him hiding from his enemies and trying to gather together enough grains of wheat to feed his family. But when an angel was sent by God to appear to him, the angel's statements reflected God's destiny for Gideon, not his meager current existence:

> **And the angel of the LORD appeared unto him, and said unto him, The LORD is with thee, thou mighty man of valour.**
>
> Judges 6:12

This language, of course, shocked and dismayed Gideon, and he wondered aloud how it could be that God was with Him. If God was with him and he was such a mighty man of valor, why was he so oppressed by the Midianites at the moment? But when Gideon realized that this was no normal visitor, the words spoken began to take hold in his spirit, and slowly he became what the angel had said he was. He rallied the troops and defeated the superior forces of the enemy, and consequently became Israel's next judge.

Take a note from this example, and start speaking destiny over your children. When your daughter lies to you, take her in your arms and say to her, "Honey, I know you lied to me, but I love you and I want you to know that you are a mighty woman of God. Women of God don't lie, so I know that you won't lie again."

When your son steals, take him in your arms and say, "Son, I know you stole, but you are a mighty man of God, and mighty men of God don't steal. So I know you won't do it again."

Speak life to your children every time you get them up in the morning and every time you put them to bed at night, even before they are able to understand what you are saying. In compassion, speak what they are going to be and what they are going to do (and not what they are now), and you will see a change.

Recently a mother brought her small girl to me for prayer, saying that the child had been around so many different spirits that she had developed a terrible confusion in her mind. I told the mother to look at her child and speak peace and truth over her. "Tell her," I said, "that she is a mighty child of God." Then I prayed for the child.

Not long afterward the mother came to me and reported that since I had prayed the girl had been like a different person. But it wasn't my prayer that brought the change; it was the compassionate words of life spoken over her by her mother. Death and life are in the power of the tongue.

Passionate Confession

Even our confession must be done with passion. As we have seen, Mark 11:23 gives us the sense of speaking aloud our desires. The prayer of verse 24 could be construed as being done in silence, but verse 23 makes clear that this is not the case:

> *"whosoever shall SAY ... ,"*
> *"whosoever ... shall believe that those things that he SAITH shall come to pass ...,"*
> *"he shall have whatsoever he SAITH."*

This is not a silent meditation, but a bold verbal declaration. Say it with passion. Speak it out with genuine feeling. Let God know that you mean it. Your life follows your words.

Please don't misunderstand me. It is not always necessary to conjure up a huge blast of emotion and to present God with an award-winning speech. But we must present our decrees with desire, with caring, with concern, with feeling, and when we do, God will establish them.

Your Special Area of Compassion

Each of us has a special area in which we feel compassion as few others can feel it. This is the area of our own experience.

I mention cancer in this book more than any other sickness, and that's because I experienced it. Having thus gone through it myself, I can understand not only the physical pain cancer sufferers experience, but also the constant psychological torment that comes along with the disease. And because I know what they are going through, I can empathize with them in a way that others cannot.

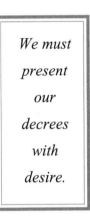

We must present our decrees with desire.

This is something that I cannot do in the natural for a drug addict, because I have never experienced it. I must ask God to allow me to feel His compassion for those who are bound by drugs.

In a very real sense, it is difficult to be effective unless and until you have been affected, and those of us who have been delivered from any sickness or bondage have a special gift that we can then share with others. Don't be surprised when people who have suffered what you suffered are drawn to you. There's a reason. And don't hesitate to reach out to them. God has drawn them to you for a purpose.

The Logical Outcome of Compassion

The outcome of Nehemiah's compassion was that God chose him to return to Jerusalem and rebuild it. The king gave him leave to go, placed in his hands letters to those who could provide materials for his work, and sent soldiers to protect him along the way. When you feel God's heartbeat, He will move heaven and earth to help you fulfill your desire. This is because your desire has become His desire, and you are fulfilling His will.

What did a cupbearer know about building a city? Probably not much, but he knew God, and he felt God's heart. This is why the compassionate of our world become the intercessors, the soul winners, the pastors of the flocks, the keepers of the food banks, the drug rehab programs, the housing centers for the homeless, the street workers, and the prison workers. Get ready; God may be calling you.

If you can feel God's compassion and learn to pray with passion about what you feel, you will quickly be praying the prayer of faith and seeing awesome results.

Chapter 8

THE NECESSARY TIMING

Behold, NOW is the accepted time; behold, NOW is the day of salvation.   2 Corinthians 6:2

The prayer of faith is a NOW prayer. It is for NOW, today, this very hour and this very moment, not for some future blessing.

Just as he does with the salvation of our souls, the enemy tries to get us to postpone, or relegate strictly to the future, our healing. If it is always future, it will never come, for tomorrow never does come.

Not Tomorrow, TODAY!

When tomorrow gets here, it will no longer be tomorrow, but today. Therefore, those who are constantly relegating their healing to the future will still be looking for it "another day," "sometime," or "in the near future." The enemy doesn't care if you believe in healing as long as you always believe in healing as a future event. If you fall for this trick, he wins every time.

This teaching touches close to home. Both a sister and a sister-in-law of mine died believing that God was going to heal them, and that really bothered me. One evening I was praying about this matter. "God, why did they die?" I asked. "Did they not believe? Was their confession not true?"

Suddenly, a light came on in my mind, as the Lord answered:

"Was their confession 'I believe I am *going to be* healed?' or was it 'I *am* healed?' " This came as a revelation to me.

When I had thought about it for a while, I realized how right the Lord was. Our healing must be brought out of the future tense and into the present, or it may never come.

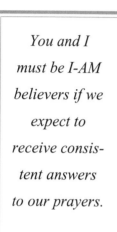

You and I must be I-AM believers if we expect to receive consistent answers to our prayers.

We never respond to the question "Are you saved?" by answering, "I believe I *will* be saved." That would be dangerous, and one might go to hell claiming it. If I asked someone the question, "Are you forgiven?" and they answered, "I believe I am *going to be* forgiven," I would worry about them. They might never be forgiven. They need to get that "going to" out of their mouth, and start making a better confession, a NOW confession.

A NOW Confession

Each of us must confess every desire we present to the Lord the same way we did it in My Decree (located on the last page of this book):

"*I* am *saved.*"
"*I* am *healed.*"
"*I* am *delivered.*"
"*I* am *protected.*"
"*I* am *made whole … in the name of Jesus.*"

"I *am!*" "I *am!*" "I *am!*" This must be your confession. "I am *going to be* saved" or "I am *going to be* healed" is not good enough. "I *am* saved," and "I *am* healed" is the only acceptable confession.

The Great I AM God

Our God is the great I AM God. When Moses asked Him what he should call Him, God told Moses to tell the children of Israel that *"I AM that I AM,"* or simply *"I AM"* had sent him (Exodus 3:14). Moses was not sent by an I-AM-GOING-TO god, and our God is not the I-AM-GOING-TO god. He is the I-AM God, the same God who blessed Moses. And you and I must be I-AM believers if we expect to receive consistent answers to our prayers.

I often hear people say, "I've confessed my healing, but I still have pain. I still have this lump in my breast, but I believe I *am going* to be healed." You don't have to *feel* healed to *be* healed; you *are* healed. So take it out of the future tense and bring it into the NOW. Your confession will become your possession.

Our God is described in His own Word as *"a very present help in trouble":*

> *God is our refuge and strength, a very present help in trouble.*
>
> Psalm 46:1

He is a present-tense God. He said:

> *I AM the Lord God and I change not.* Malachi 3:6

When Moses told the people that I AM had sent him, it meant that God was there for whatever they needed, for whatever situation might arise. He was there right then, not sometime in the distant future.

"I am going to be saved someday" is a bad confession that delights the enemy, and so is "I am going to be healed." Say "I am healed" and cling to that confession. When you do, you are speaking things that are not as though they already existed in the present. And they will.

As we have seen, that is a correct way of thinking, and it is consistent with the reality of God. He has already finished the work in your life. All you have to do is continue to confess your desire and to refuse to let go of it until you get what you are believing for.

This is *NOW* faith, as the writer of Hebrews declared:

> *NOW faith is the substance of things hoped for and the evidence of things not seen.*   Hebrews 11:1

Jesus said to the Jews of His day:

> *Before Abraham was, I AM.*   John 8:58

The men He was addressing that day were Abraham's descendants, and they were rightfully proud of the patriarch. But God wanted them to know that before the great Abraham was, He is.

He is the God of today, and you can have your blessing today, not tomorrow. A proper confession is always a NOW confession because God is always a NOW God.

If you can take your confession out of the future and bring it into the present, you are ready to pray the prayer of faith with power and get results.

Chapter 9

THE NECESSARY NAME

And whatsoever ye shall ask IN MY NAME, that will I do, that
the Father may be glorified in the Son. If ye shall ask any thing
IN MY NAME, I will do it.   John 14:13-14

The prayer of faith is always made in the name of Jesus and in no
other name. It is His name that is powerful, not yours, or mine, or
someone else's. James made this very clear:

> *Is any sick among you? let him call for the elders of the church;*
> *and let them pray over him, anointing him with oil IN THE*
> *NAME OF THE LORD.*   James 5:14

No part of the healing ministry is done in our own name or in
our own strength. We lay hands on the sick in the name of Jesus,
and we speak healing to them in the name of Jesus. "In the name
of Jesus, you are healed," are words, which spoken with the proper
power and authority, will create the desired healing.

The healing is not in our hands. Our hands just become a me-
dium through which God's life pours from heaven to earth.
Therefore we can lay hands on the sick without fear. We are doing
it IN JESUS' NAME.

The words of life that we speak are not our words; they are His.
And, because they are His, we can speak them without fear. His
words break the power of Satan, death, and demons, and He has

given us the authority to do that same thing through the use of His name.

We Have the Power To Use His Name Because We Have Been Deputized

Healing was a major part of the ministry of Jesus. Here are just a few examples from the Scriptures:

And his fame went throughout all Syria: and they brought unto him all sick people that were taken with divers diseases and torments, and those which were possessed with devils, and those which were lunatic, and those that had the palsy; and HE HEALED THEM.   Matthew 4:24

Great multitudes followed him, and HE HEALED THEM ALL.   Matthew 12:15

And great multitudes came unto him, having with them those that were lame, blind, dumb, maimed, and many others, and cast them down at Jesus' feet; and HE HEALED THEM: insomuch that the multitude wondered, when they saw the dumb to speak, the maimed to be whole, the lame to walk, and the blind to see: and they glorified the God of Israel.   Matthew 15:30-31

And great multitudes followed him; and HE HEALED THEM there.   Matthew 19:2

And the blind and the lame came to him in the temple; and HE HEALED THEM.   Matthew 21:14

The Necessary Name

This same healing power was then transferred to the disciples. He gathered them together and deputized them to act in His stead, much as a sheriff did with a wild West posse:

> *Then he called his twelve disciples together, and gave them POWER AND AUTHORITY over all devils, and TO CURE DISEASES. And he sent them to preach the kingdom of God, and to HEAL THE SICK.* Luke 9:1-2

Because the power of God was being transferred to these men, they could now act in Jesus' stead, or in His name. And, when they acted, they would be acting on His behalf. Therefore, they had His full authority. That's really what it means to do something *"in Jesus' name."*

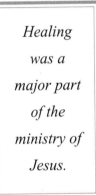

Healing was a major part of the ministry of Jesus.

This truth impacted me so much that we made up a miniature sheriff's badge containing the promise of Luke 9:1 and had it duplicated. Then I began to take these with me wherever I ministered and used them to "deputize" God's people.

I had people raise their right hand and repeat after me:

> *I do solemnly affirm that from this day forward I will go forth with power and authority, according to Luke 9:1, to destroy the works of the enemy, to heal the sick and set the captives free, and to recover all that Satan has stolen from me.*
>
> *In the name of Jesus.*

Then I would tell them, "Now you are deputized. Go forth and do the work God has commissioned you to do. It was all very powerful and moving, and people loved it.

I also love that badge because it reminds me of who I am in Christ, and so I wear one myself. I'm not nearly as interested in impressing people with it as I am of reminding myself of the authority I have in Christ according to Luke 9:1.

The badge has become a conversation piece, as many people see it and ask about its significance. At first, I wasn't sure exactly what to say when people saw me wearing it in public places (like airports) and asked me, "Are you a sheriff?"

After a few times, I learned to answer, "No, but this is my badge of authority." And that has opened many doors for me to witness to perfect strangers.

The seventy men Jesus sent forth were deputized in the same way, and their authority to act on Jesus' behalf, or in His name, worked for them:

> *And the seventy returned again with joy, saying, Lord, even the devils are subject unto us THROUGH THY NAME.*
>
> Luke 10:17

This worked for Peter and the other disciples even after Jesus was gone. For example:

> *Then Peter said, Silver and gold have I none; but such as I have give I thee: IN THE NAME OF JESUS CHRIST OF NAZA-RETH rise up and walk. And he took him by the right hand, and lifted him up: and immediately his feet and ankle bones received strength. And he leaping up stood, and walked, and entered with them into the temple, walking, and leaping, and praising God.*
>
> Acts 3:6-8

You and I have been deputized in this same way, and using the authority of the name of Jesus that has been given to us will bring results for us today as well. Just before He returned to heaven, Jesus spoke of signs that would follow *"them that believe"* and act in His name:

> *And these signs shall follow them that believe; IN MY NAME shall they cast out devils; they shall speak with new tongues. ⋯ They shall lay hands on the sick, and they shall recover.*
>
> Mark 16:17-18

Are you among those who believe? Then you are deputized, and thus authorized, to use the name of our Lord Jesus.

The Power Behind This Name

God has chosen to honor the name of His Son Jesus and make it the name of all power and authority:

> *Therefore God also has highly exalted Him and given Him the name which is above every name, that at the name of Jesus every knee should bow, of those in heaven, and of those on earth, and of those under the earth, and that every tongue should confess that Jesus Christ is Lord, to the glory of God the Father.*
>
> Philippians 2:9-11

We, therefore, are to *"do all"* in His name:

> *And whatsoever ye do in word or deed, DO ALL IN THE NAME OF THE LORD JESUS, giving thanks to God and the Father by him.* Colossians 3:17

Of course, we can use the name of Jesus with authority only when we are in good standing with Him, when we are doing all that we can to know and obey His will, and when we are speaking His words.

Under any other circumstances, it simply will not work. Empty words never bear fruit.

When some Jewish men of Paul's day (who were said to be *"exorcists"*) saw him using the name of Jesus with success, they decided to try it themselves. The results were disastrous for them:

When we speak our desire and we do it in His name, it is as if He is speaking, so it will *come to pass.*

Then certain of the vagabond Jews, exorcists, took upon them to call over them which had evil spirits THE NAME OF THE LORD JESUS, saying, We adjure you BY JESUS whom Paul preacheth. And there were seven sons of one Sceva, a Jew, and chief of the priests, which did so. And the evil spirit answered and said, JESUS I know, and Paul I know; but who are ye? And the man in whom the evil spirit was leaped on them, and overcame them, and prevailed against them, so that they fled out of that house naked and wounded.

Acts 19:13-16

Of course demons know Jesus, and they knew Paul because he was legally deputized to act on the Lord's behalf. But the other men were clearly acting on their own, and their words, however correct, meant nothing at all. When you use the name of Jesus, make sure that you are His and that He has given you the authority to use the name which is above all other names.

The Source of My Own Authority

I dropped out of high school in the eleventh grade to marry Lawrence, and when I felt called to the ministry, people told me that I could never preach. There were other reasons besides my not having finished high school. "You've never been to seminary," some reminded me, and others said, "You've never been ordained."

But I knew what God had said to me. He had called me to do His work, and I was to do it in His name, not my own, and with His authority, not my own. While there is nothing wrong with education and ordination, neither of them can be our source of authority.

God ordained Jeremiah from the womb as a prophet to the nations:

Before I formed thee in the belly I knew thee; and before thou camest forth out of the womb I sanctified thee, and I ORDAINED THEE a prophet unto the nations.　　　Jeremiah 1:5

Jeremiah had not yet been ordained by an earthly organization, and he had not yet completed his seminary training. How could he? He wasn't even born yet. This may be an extreme case, but none of us can afford to rely only on authority given to use through a certificate or through a ceremony. Real authority only comes from God.

It was He who ordained me to the ministry, and He who helped me to gain an understanding of the sacred Scriptures. Because of that, I know who I am, and I know that God is on my side.

And, if God is for me, who can be against me? I am acting in His name, and I do it with His full authority. He said:

Ye have not chosen me, but I have chosen you, and ordained you, that ye should go and bring forth fruit, and that your fruit should remain: that whatsoever ye shall ask of the Father IN MY NAME, he may give it you.　　　John 15:16

When we speak our desire and we do it in His name, it is as if He is speaking, so it *will* come to pass. Every prayer, therefore, must be based on His will and on His Words, and be uttered in His name. And the results are assured:

> *And in that day ye shall ask me nothing. Verily, verily, I say unto you, Whatsoever ye shall ask the Father IN MY NAME, he will give it you. Hitherto have ye asked nothing IN MY NAME: ask, and ye shall receive, that your joy may be full.*
>
> John 16:23-24

So, what more needs to be said? If you learn the authority of the name of Jesus and you learn to use it in a way pleasing to Him, you are ready to pray the prayer of faith with power and effectiveness.

Chapter 10

THE NECESSARY REMEMBERING

Do ye not REMEMBER?   Mark 8:18

The prayer of faith is a prayer of remembering. This thought may need some explaining.

After Jesus had fed the five thousand, He told His disciples to get into a boat and cross the sea toward Bethsaida. He would dismiss the people who had come for His teachings, and then He would follow the disciples. As they started obediently across the sea, He went up to a mountain to pray. And, then, as nightfall set in, He somehow saw them struggling to survive in the middle of a sea that had turned angry.

This was quite miraculous because (1) It was night, and one could not see that far at night, and (2) The sea was quite wide, and it would have been very difficult, if not totally impossible, for someone to see clearly from a mountain on the shore what was happening in the middle of the sea. That would have been difficult in full daylight. Still, although these men thought they were alone, Jesus saw them toiling, and He came to them.

This was one of the occasions when Jesus appeared to them walking on the sea. They saw Him and thought it was a ghost, but He got into the boat with them:

> *And he went up unto them into the ship; and the wind ceased: and they were sore amazed in themselves beyond measure, and wondered.*   Mark 6:51

YOUR LIFE FOLLOWS YOUR WORDS

Think about it! These disciples had just seen Jesus feed five thousand men with their women and children, and now they were amazed and could not believe what they were seeing. Why was that? The Scriptures say, *"Their heart was hardened"*:

> *For they considered not the miracle of the loaves: for THEIR HEART WAS HARDENED.*   Mark 6:52

Later, Jesus fed four thousand (see Mark 8:9). Again, He and the disciples got into a ship and were leaving when the disciples realized that they had forgotten to bring any bread with them. They had only *"one loaf"* in the boat (verse 14). When Jesus heard them reasoning about the lack of bread, He said to them:

> *Why reason ye, because ye have no bread? perceive ye not yet, neither understand? have ye your heart yet hardened? having eyes, see ye not? and having ears, hear ye not? and DO YE NOT REMEMBER?*   Mark 8:17-18

Remembering is a powerful tool that can keep us through life's storms.

He asked them how many basketfuls of bread had been left over after He had fed the five thousand, and they answered twelve. He asked them how many basketfuls had been left over after He had fed the four thousand, and they said seven. So, He said to them:

> *How is it that ye do not understand?*   Mark 8:21

If He had done this once, and, in fact, He had already done it more than once, was there any reason to believe that He could not do it again? They needed to remember: *"DO YE NOT REMEMBER?"*

The Necessary Remembering

Remembering Is a Powerful Tool

Remembering is a powerful tool that can keep us through life's storms. Some who have been rescued from the pits or the hog pens of this world by our Lord have returned to their former life because they forgot what God had done for them. I have known people who were healed of serious illnesses by God, only to backslide and go to hell. They forgot what the Lord had done.

In Old Testament days, God placed memorials in strategic places to remind His people of the miracles they had received at His hands. He warned them:

> *Take heed unto yourselves, LEST YE FORGET ... .*
> Deuteronomy 4:23

Passover is just such a memorial, the other feasts initiated by the Lord for the people of Israel were also memorials. The contents of the Ark of the covenant were very strong memorials of three occasions when God had done great miracles for them. God told them to set up a simple memorial with stones at the point of the crossing of the Jordan so that they would remember their miraculous crossing of it. And there were other similar memorials. Each one would remind them (and future generations) of the goodness of the Lord.

Although we cannot live in the past, we should never forget where God has brought us from. Every battle you win should become a stepping stone to victory in the next battle. The enemy wants you to forget, but God wants you to remember. And we should also want to remember. What He did for us in the last test will carry us through the next one too, so we cannot afford to forget:

> *Only take heed to thyself, and keep thy soul diligently, LEST THOU FORGET the things which thine eyes have seen, and*

YOUR LIFE FOLLOWS YOUR WORDS

LEST THEY DEPART FROM THY HEART all the days of thy life: but teach them thy sons, and thy sons' sons.

Deuteronomy 4:9

Peter was aware of this necessity to remember:

Wherefore I will not be negligent to put you always in REMEM-BRANCE of these things, though ye know them, and be established in the present truth. Yea, I think it meet, as long as I am in this tabernacle, to stir you up by putting you IN REMEMBRANCE.

2 Peter 1:12-13

This second epistle, beloved, I now write unto you; in both which I stir up your pure minds BY WAY OF REMEMBRANCE.

2 Peter 3:1

It doesn't matter how firmly we are *"established in the truth,"* we still need to remember. Causing us to forget is one of the greatest weapons the enemy has at his disposal. This is the reason that we are to enter into the presence of the Lord with a thankful heart. Our attitude of remembering and giving thanks prepares the way for more miracles to come to our lives.

As children of God, we should think of ways to help ourselves remember. One thing we can do is to record His goodness in a diary or journal. Later, we can read it over, and others can read it too. Books are another good way of establishing memorials to the Lord. We have all been blessed by some good ones.

Another thing you might do is to write down in the blank pages of your Bible some of the great things God has done for you. There won't be enough pages to hold them, but what you can write will be helpful—to you and to succeeding generations. I have just such a Bible that I trust will one day bless my grandchildren and challenge them to have faith in God.

Another thing I do is to keep an actual basket at home, and in it I have some of the loaves of artificial bread readily available in stores these days. On the bottom of each loaf that I place there, I write what miracle it stands for. My basket and the loaves of bread in it remind me of what God has done for us in the past. Here are just a few examples:

Jana Was Healed of a Deformity

Our daughter Jana, who now is the Minister of Music and Choir Director of our church, was born with a deformity in her body. The ligaments on one side of her neck were only half the size of those on the other side, and therefore she couldn't carry her head straight. One side of her face was also smaller than the other. It was pitiful to see her with her little head cocked at an angle, one side nearly leaned over on her shoulder.

A specialist in Cincinnati told me that there was nothing that could be done surgically for her. "She will never be normal," the doctor said. "She will always carry her head that way."

Jana was my first baby, and this was devastating news. As I left the doctor's office that day, I began to rebuke the enemy and pray and seek God for an answer. One night, not long afterward, we had already gone to bed when a knock came on the door. It was Lawrence's father.

"God sent me," he said, "to pray for Jana. Let me in."

Lawrence opened the door, and his father went straight to the baby's room, got her up out of her bed, and began to pray. "Devil," he said, "you take your hands off of this baby. She's healed."

And she was healed. She was immediately able to hold her head up straight, and the smallness in one side of her face evened out over the next few months, until no one could tell that she had ever had the problem.

I wrote that miracle in my Bible so that I would never forget it, and so that my children, grandchildren, and great-grandchildren would never forget it. And I made that one of the loaves in my basket that help me never to forget God's goodness.

Lawrence, II Was Healed of a Birth Defect and of Serious Asthma

Our son Lawrence was born without a tear duct, and one of his eyes would mat up so badly at night that it took a long time to clean it out enough each morning so that he could get his eye open. The tears also kept one spot on his face raw. The doctor said that he could surgically implant a tear duct later if we wanted him to.

One evening I was playing the piano at church, and someone brought Lawrence and placed him in my arms because he was a little fussy. I looked down at his face and saw that raw place, and I cried out to God. "You created every cell of this baby's body, God, and I know that You can make him a tear duct."

That was all I said, but the next morning I kept thinking that there was something I was forgetting to do. Finally, I remembered that I hadn't gotten Lawrence's eye open yet. I ran to his room, but to my delight, that eye was already opened. God had given our son a tear duct, and he didn't have to go back to the doctor.

I wrote that miracle down in my Bible so that I would never forget and so that others could read it and be blessed as well. And it became one of the loaves in my basket that helps me to remember what God has done for us.

Lawrence was also born with a form of asthma. "Some forms of asthma improve with age," his doctor told us, "but this particular kind will get worse with time. He will probably never have a normal life because of it, and it may, at some point, destroy his lungs and end his life early."

When Lawrence got to the age that he wanted to run and play, he had a hard time breathing, and he had to exert himself so much that his body would be covered with perspiration and his hair soaked. Still, the more we tried to restrain him, the more he wanted to run. It bothered him that he could not be like other children.

We kept an oxygen tent that he slept in at night, but we still made occasional visits with him to the Emergency Room when he had severe asthma attacks.

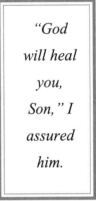

"God will heal you, Son," I assured him.

"God will heal you, Son," I assured him, "and then you'll be able to run and play like a normal child. And you won't need this tent anymore or your visits to the Emergency Room."

He was eight when he got into a prayer line one night, was prayed for, and never had another asthma attack. He said it felt like someone had pulled two socks out of his lungs. His airways had opened up. He can do anything he wants to do, and it doesn't bother him.

I will never forget that miracle because I wrote it down in my Bible, and it's one of the loaves of bread in my basket that help me to remember God's unfailing goodness.

Renee Was Healed of Severe Burns

When our daughter Renee was two, she pulled a bowl of hot bacon grease off of the stove onto her face and body. I had cooked a pound of bacon and had just placed the hot grease from it in a bowl beside the stove when she reached up and pulled it over on herself.

The hot grease took the skin off of her little face. It ran down her leg, and when we quickly pulled her pants off of her, the skin came with them.

"Because she's a baby," we were told at the hospital, "her scars may not be as bad, but she *will* be scarred." But, as God is my witness, Renee does not have a trace of a scar.

I wrote this miracle down for my remembrance and for the sake of all those who would come after me, and it is also one of the loaves in my basket of remembrance.

I Was Healed of Breast Cancer

In 1986, I was preparing to do a women's conference at one of our local churches here in Ohio. I had been preaching for many weeks a series of messages on faith, and God was doing many wonderful things for us. Because of it, the devil was angry—very angry.

One night, after I had taken a bath, I was lying in my bed meditating on the Lord, and I heard a voice that said, "If you don't stop, I'm going to kill you."

It was so real that I responded immediately. "Devil, you're not big enough!"

"Well, feel your right breast," he urged.

I had just bathed, and I knew that there was nothing there, but now the first spot I touched on my right breast was sore. As I examined myself a little more, I quickly found a lump in that breast the size of a silver dollar. In that moment, it seemed that every ounce of faith left me. I went into the bathroom, and I stayed there most of the night weeping and complaining to God.

"Why *me*, God?" I sobbed.

"Why would You allow the devil to attack me in this way? I've been saved for as long as I can remember—all of my life practically. All I have ever wanted in life was to serve You. I've done everything I knew to do for You ... and now this."

It was exactly the wrong thing to do. Whining, murmuring, and complaining have never gotten God's attention. I sometimes wonder if He even hears us when we are talking out of our own self-pity. I was devastated by what I had found, but this was no way to get rid of it.

The next day I never left my room. I had to tell Lawrence why, but I made him promise me that he would not tell anyone else.

After I had spent three days in rather bitter seclusion, Lawrence, II, who was then about twenty, came into my room. "Mom, what in the world is wrong with you?" he asked. "This is not like you. You haven't been out of this bedroom for three days."

"Honey," I said, "the enemy has attacked me, and I will not leave this room until the Lord heals me." And that *was* my determination

"I don't want to tell anyone about this until it's over," I continued. "Then I'll tell all of you what had been going on."

"Mom," he insisted, "I am not leaving this room until you tell me what's wrong."

With that, my defenses crumbled, and I broke down and began to cry and told him exactly what had happened.

He listened patiently to what I had to say, and then he began to speak to me. He did it very respectfully and sweetly, but he also did it firmly.

"Mom," he said, "can I ask you something?"

"Yes, Honey, you can," I responded.

"You told me that I was born without a tear duct, but that you prayed for me one night in church, and that God healed me. Is that the truth?"

"It is," I assured him.

He went on: "I remember the problems I had with asthma as a young kid, but you always told me that God was going to heal me.

Because of that faith, I got into a prayer line when I was eight, and God instantly healed me."

"I know it, Honey," I said. "I will never forget it."

"Well," he continued, "you've been preaching to our people for weeks now that God can do anything, that nothing is impossible when we trust Him. Do you believe what you've been telling them? Or has it just been empty words?"

"No!" I assured him, "I believe what I've been preaching."

> *Do you believe what you've been preaching? Or has it just been empty words?*

"Well, then I want you to get up and get out of this bedroom because the devil is never going to be able to kill you. God is not finished with you yet. So, get up and get your makeup on, and get out of this house—please." And he left.

Lawrence's words echoed over and over to me after he had left my room, and slowly my faith began to return. He had caused me to remember, and that remembering had strengthened my faith that God had not changed. If He had done miracles for us in the past, He would do miracles for us again.

I stood in my bathroom and boldly proclaimed, "Devil, get out your little black book and write this down. I don't want you to ever forget what God's going to do for me. I'm going to show you that the Word of God that I have been preaching is the same Word that I stand on and live by. God is going to heal me, and there will be no other acceptable outcome to this situation."

When I had finished proclaiming all that I needed to proclaim I expected the lump to be gone, and I was surprised when it wasn't. It was still there the next day and the next, and the next week, and the next month, and it had gotten progressively worse. Now, the

entire lower half of my breast had become a solid mass. The sore-
ness I originally discovered turned into pain, and the pain increased
in severity until it seemed like someone was sticking hot coals of
fire into my flesh, as if someone had stuck a knife clear through
me.

I had always been rather closemouthed about my personal ailments. Whenever I was not feeling well, no one heard me complain
about it. Lawrence and the children usually didn't even know about
it until it was over. I had always gone to God, and He had healed
me. Now I sensed that I needed help in prayer. I selected seven
women from our church in whom I could confide, and I made
them covenant with me that they would not discuss this matter with
others, but would pray with me for my healing every day.

As the pain became so unbearable that it was difficult for me to
sleep, I would get up, go into the bathroom and find a good scriptural promise that I could cling to through the night. I wrote these
down, went over them a few times, and then kept a piece of paper
with the verse written on it in my hand the rest of the night, turning to it as I needed it for consolation and assurance.

For instance, I used Psalm 118:17:

> *I shall not die, but live, and declare the works of the LORD.*
> Psalm 118:17

When I would wake up in pain, I would declare, "It is written, *'I
shall not die, but live, and declare the works of the LORD.'* " Then I would
be able to sleep again.

Sometimes I would have to get up and quote scripture for a while,
and then I could go back to bed and sleep some more.

Then lumps appeared under my arm, and the breast began to
bleed. After several weeks of this, the bleeding had advanced to
the point that I needed to keep absorbent pads in my bra over that

breast like those used by mothers who are breast-feeding so that the blood would not come through onto my clothes. Often I would get up in the middle of the night and find my nightgown drenched in blood and have to go to the bathroom and wash it off.

One day I was praying with the seven women in the church. By that time, my breast was bleeding so badly that it seemed like a water faucet. I pulled the bra back for them to see, and blood ran down. "God," I prayed, "You're still God. I am healed."

On the night of July 21, I bled so badly that the next morning the blood was on my sheets and had soaked through to the mattress. Lawrence's mother Mary was staying with us and helping me take care of the house at the time, but I didn't want her to see this and be alarmed. I got up, took off the sheets, and quickly threw them into the washing machine. Then I went to the bathroom to clean myself up.

This had gone on now for five months, and no end was in sight. I stood there at the sink with tears splashing down into the bloody water, and I said, "God, even if this breast rots and falls off into this water, I am still going to preach that You are Jehovah-Rophe, the Lord who heals me. What's going on in this body doesn't change the fact that You are still the Healer. I will believe it and preach it until the very last breath leaves my body."

In that instant, I heard God call my name. If I had ever heard the audible voice of the Lord, it was that day.

"Darlene," he said.

I raised my head. "Yes, Lord."

He said, "Because you have not leaned on the arm of the flesh but have continued to trust in My Word, and because you have continued to confess in the face of the bleeding and the pain that I am your Healer, as of this day you are healed. Go and proclaim it."

And I was healed. The bleeding and the pain stopped instantly, within three days the breast returned to normal, and I have been well since then.

I wrote this miracle down as a memorial, and I put another loaf of bread into my basket. I didn't want to ever forget, and I didn't want others to ever forget either.

God Healed My Mother

One day in 1990 my father called with some bad news about my mother. "Darlene," he said, "we just got back from the doctors in Nashville, and they say there is nothing they can do for your mother. If you want to see her alive, you need to come quickly. She's so bad off that she can't walk across the room by herself."

Mama had asthma, the same type of asthma Lawrence, II had been born with, the same type of asthma the doctors had said might kill him when he got older, and now her condition had suddenly worsened.

"Let me talk to her," I said.

My mother, who had lost seventy-five percent of her hearing, got on the phone, and I spoke loud enough so that she could hear me.

"What did the doctors say?" I asked.

"They said that my lungs are in very bad shape, and that the polyps in my head (her sinus cavities were filled with polyps) are so full of infection that they don't know what else to do for me."

"Well, you know that God can heal you," I assured.

"Yes," she replied, "but I'm so tired. I've always been an active person, a hard worker, but now I can't even vacuum my own floor. I can't walk across the room without giving out. I just don't want to live like this. I think I would rather go on and be with the Lord."

"Mama, stop talking like that," I urged. "You're only sixty-six, and that's not old enough to die. Besides, your family needs you.

"You know what God did for me just a few years ago when He

147

healed my breast. You know how He healed Jana's neck." And, in this way, I began to rehearse in my mother's hearing some of the many miracles God had done for our family through the years. One by one, I picked up the loaves from my basket and reminded her of them. Because I had them, I could now help someone else.

Many years before this, Mother had lost her sense of smell. She wore a fragrance called Ciara, and she wore it so strong that it was overpowering to others, simply because she couldn't smell it herself.

Along with the loss of her sense of smell, she had also lost her sense of taste, and her severe hearing loss was more troubling than ever. During her last visit to my house, she had sat some ten feet away as I was preparing a meal, and as loud as I could shout, she was unable to hear me well enough to carry on a decent conversation. "I just can't hear anymore," she had lamented that day.

"Let me just go on," she insisted now.

"No," I said, "you can't do that. You're too young. Please," Mama, I urged, "if you'll do what I tell you, you'll be healed."

"Well, what do you want me to do?" she asked.

I had been praying about what to tell her, and suddenly I knew.

"Doctors have said there was no more they could do. Is that right?" I began.

"Yes," she agreed.

"Then, here's the first thing you need to do," I said. "Get together all of your medications, and then dump them into the toilet and flush them away." * Make sure you're following the Lord. I'm not telling you to stop taking your medication. This is what the Lord told me for this particular situation.

"But I've been on steroids for a long time," my mother objected, "and they always say that if you ever come off of them, you need to do it slowly."

"Mama," what I'm telling you now is from the Lord," I insisted. "I wouldn't tell you to do that if He hadn't said it specifically."

"Okay, I'll do it," she promised.

"Next," I continued, "when you get up each morning, I want you to read Psalm 131. At noon, I want you to read Psalm 103." I gave her another scripture to read at three P.M. and another to read a 6 P.M. "If you will take *this* medicine as faithfully as you have taken your other medications, God will heal you," I promised. And I knew He would.

But no sooner had I hung up the telephone than the devil jumped on me. What if the things I had told Mama to do caused some bad reaction? I spent a restless night, and the devil kept saying to me, "Your mama's going to die, and your brothers will sue you for killing her."

Just as early as I dared, I called my parent's home. Dad answered as usual.

"How's Mama doing?" I asked.

"She seems to be about the same," he said.

The next morning, when I called, his report hadn't changed: "She might be breathing a little easier, but I'm not sure. I can't tell much difference."

But seven or eight days later, he called me a little agitated and a lot excited. "Darlene," he said, "I want to know what you did to your mother."

"Why, Dad?" I asked.

"Because suddenly she wants everything that has needed to be done for the past two years to be done today."

"So she's doing better?" I asked.

"She is, but she's killing me in the process," he complained.

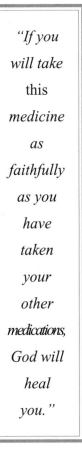

"If you will take this *medicine as faithfully as you have taken your other medications, God will heal you."*

About two weeks later, Mom called me.

"Honey, do you know what I did today?" she asked.

"What, Mother?" I asked.

She said, "I vacuumed the floor, and after I got done vacuuming the floor I went out and mowed two acres of grass on the riding mower." We rejoiced together.

Three weeks later, the phone rang one morning just after daylight, and I heard Mama's voice on the other end of the line. She was obviously excited. "Honey," she said, "I knew you would be sleeping, but it was so good that I couldn't keep it. You know how my sense of smell has been lost for so many years?"

"Sure, Mom," I said.

"Well, you won't believe what woke me up this morning."

"What was it, Mama?" I asked.

"I smelled the coffee your daddy was making in the kitchen, and the smell woke me up," was her reply.

"But that's not the best part of it," she continued. "I got up and fixed biscuits and gravy, and they haven't tasted so good in twenty years."

"But that's still not the very best part," she insisted as I rejoiced. "I can hear now as well as I did when I was a teenager."

My mother sounded like a new woman; she clearly had a new lease on life. She is now eighty, and is still strong and alert, and she has never again had a recurrence of her asthma.

That's a miracle worth remembering, and it tells me that our God hasn't changed and that He will do the same thing today.

What About Your Loaves?

These are some of the miracles that God has done in my family, but I'm sure that He has done great things for you too. After all, He is *"no respecter of persons"*:

150

The Necessary Remembering

Then Peter opened his mouth, and said, Of a truth I perceive that God is NO RESPECTER OF PERSONS: but in every nation he that feareth him, and worketh righteousness, is accepted with him.   Acts 10:34-35

Don't forget about your loaves. Keep them fresh. Keep retelling your stories, your testimonies. Keep remembering and reminding others of what God has done, and you will keep receiving miracles from His hand every day.

Give God the praise. You already have lots of loaves in your basket, and you are expecting to receive many more at His hand. Take a moment to praise Him right now for all of your past and future victories.

Another Important Element of Our Remembering

There is another important element of our remembering. It is not only important to remind ourselves, but it is also important to remind God.

"Remind God?" some might ask. "What's that all about?"

Well God likes us to remind Him of His promises. He said:

Put me IN REMEMBRANCE.   Isaiah 43:26

This means that we can search the Scriptures, find a promise that fits our need, and then stand on it. We can speak it out—not only ourselves, but also to God.

"But isn't that offensive to the Lord?" I imagine some asking.

No, it's not; He actually likes it.

Recently a woman in our congregation came up to me and said, "I want to remind you of something you said to me that you may have forgotten. You told me that when I had lost a hundred pounds, you would buy me a new dress. Well, I have lost *two* hundred pounds."

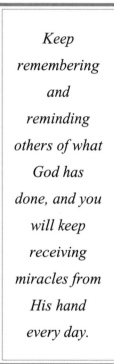

Keep remembering and reminding others of what God has done, and you will keep receiving miracles from His hand every day.

I honestly didn't remember having told her that, but I must have, so I said I would do it. Always very helpful, Lawrence chimed in, "You'll have to buy her *two* new dresses because she lost *twice* as much as you bargained for."

It didn't bother me to be reminded of my promise, and it didn't bother me to buy the sister a new dress—or even two. I was happy for her. And this is how our Lord feels when we are blessed. So don't hesitate to remind Him of His promises to you. This is another great incentive for us to study His Word and learn well all that He has promised.

Then say to Him, "Hey, God. I found something today. I found my promise. It is written, and I will confess it from this day forward until I receive it. Because You said it, and You cannot lie and are a debtor to no man, I am expecting it to happen."

And it will, for our God never fails.

When you have done the necessary remembering, you are ready to pray with effectiveness the prayer of faith.

---

* Please see the disclaimer on the copyright page.

Chapter 11

THE NECESSARY EXAMPLE

And he said, Young man, I say unto thee, Arise.   Luke 7:14

The prayer of faith is a prayer we can learn to pray effectively through following Jesus' good example.

As with everything else in the Christian life, Jesus is our very best example when it comes to knowing how to minister to the sick and suffering. Therefore, as we look more closely at the examples of His prayers found recorded in the Scriptures, they can teach us what *our* prayers should be like.

Jesus' prayers were not wordy or eloquent. In fact, they were amazingly short and simple. His prayers were powerful and faith-filled, never weak and doubt ridden. In His prayers, He never mentioned the problem He was addressing. Refusing to consider the circumstances surrounding the situation He wanted to change, He only prayed the end result He (and His Father) desired to receive. Consequently, He always received answers, and they came very quickly.

Jesus' Faith-Filled Words

As an example, when Jesus saw a widow in Nain preparing to bury her son, He refused to consider the fact that her child was already dead, lying in a coffin, and on the way to his burial plot. He refused to consider the fact that mourners filled the streets, weeping and bemoaning the son' death. All He could think of was the Father's will that this man live.

When Jesus acted, His actions were positive, and when He spoke, His words were both positive and life-giving. To the mother, He said, *"Weep not,"* and to the dead man, He said, *"Young man, I say unto thee, Arise."* That's all He said, but it was enough:

> *And it came to pass the day after, that he went into a city called Nain; and many of his disciples went with him, and much people. Now when he came nigh to the gate of the city, behold, there was a dead man carried out, the only son of his mother, and she was a widow: and much people of the city was with her. And when the Lord saw her, he had compassion on her, and said unto her, Weep not. And he came and touched the bier: and they that bare him stood still. And he said, Young man, I say unto thee, Arise. And he that was dead sat up, and began to speak. And he delivered him to his mother. And there came a fear on all: and they glorified God, saying, That a great prophet is risen up among us; and, That God hath visited his people. And this rumour of him went forth throughout all Judaea, and throughout all the region round about. And the disciples of John showed him of all these things.*
>
> Luke 7:11-18

When Jesus prayed, He didn't waste words. He just demanded the end result He desired, calling those things that were not as though they were, and believing for the answer. And it always came.

In another example, when Jesus encountered a leper, He again refused to speak of the problem. Rather, He touched the leper's hand and spoke healing to him:

The Necessary Example

And he put forth his hand, and touched him, saying, I WILL: BE THOU CLEAN. And immediately the leprosy departed from him.   Luke 5:13

"I will: be thou clean." Five words. That's all that Jesus said to the man, and yet the desired miracle came.

When our Lord encountered blind Bartimaeus, it was a similar scene:

And Jesus said unto him, GO THY WAY; THY FAITH HATH MADE THEE WHOLE. And immediately he received his sight, and followed Jesus in the way.   Mark 10:52

Jesus didn't even take time to rebuke the blindness that had afflicted Bartimaeus. He spoke few words, only nine, and yet *"immediately"* the needed miracle came.

When Jesus encountered a man with a withered hand, He spoke only four words— *"stretch forth thy hand"*:

Then saith he to the man, STRETCH FORTH THINE HAND. And he stretched it forth; and it was restored whole, like as the other.   Matthew 12:13

"Stretch forth thine hand!" That's all He said, and yet I can somehow see the man stretching out his hand for the first time. I see him beginning to straighten one finger, then another, and then another ... until his hand was made perfectly whole.

Why was the man able to do this? Because Jesus spoke words that were packed with so much faith and power that they

> *When Jesus spoke, His words were positive and life-giving.*

created the miracle in the man's life. That withered hand could not remain abnormal, because Jesus had spoken what was not and caused it to be.

There are many other examples that we could cite, but these are enough to show the pattern of Jesus' prayers of faith and their results.

Jesus' Words Are Spirit and Life

Jesus said of His words:

> *The WORDS that I speak unto you, they are SPIRIT, and they are LIFE.*   John 6:63

As we have noted, very often we are defeated because the devil speaks death into our situation, and we believe him. We then go on to speak what we have experienced and not what God has to say about our specific situation. Instead of saying what the devil prompts us to say about our situations, we need to say what God has to say about them, for His words are spirit and life. So, when we pray, we must pray the desired end result, His will for the situation, not the current condition. This was what Jesus did.

Jesus encountered some blind men who desired to be healed, and it is interesting to see what He told them:

> *And when he was come into the house, the blind men came to him: and Jesus saith unto them, Believe ye that I am able to do this? They said unto him, Yea, Lord. Then touched he their eyes, saying, ACCORDING TO YOUR FAITH BE IT UNTO YOU. And their eyes were opened.*   Matthew 9:28-30

"According to your faith be it unto you." The meaning conveyed by

the original Greek text here is: *"Your reward shall be equal to your faith"* (Rieu). It's not that God cannot or does not heal, for it is clearly not His will that any should perish. Jesus had the faith, and His words were spirit and life, and the rest was up to the blind men.

Creative Words

God created this world and everything in it just by speaking the Word. He spoke, and the worlds began to turn. He didn't have to call a lumber company and order materials. He created everything that now exists out of nothing. His words were creative.

When a desire came into the heart of God to create a man that He could love, He said:

Let us make man in our own image, and in our own likeness.
Genesis 1:21

Then God scooped up some earth, and from it, He made Adam in His image and likeness, just as He had desired. He didn't need to call for a plastic surgeon or a molecular scientist and ask them how it should be done. He knew what He desired, He spoke out His desire, and it was.

And it didn't take him millions of years to accomplish it. In a moment's time, His desire was fulfilled. He spoke it, and it existed.

These principles, set forth in example by God Himself and demonstrated to us through Jesus when He was on earth, can also be exercised by mortal men. Joshua, for example, exercised this principle when he told the sun to stand still:

Then spake Joshua ... , and he said in the sight of Israel, SUN, STAND THOU STILL UPON GIBEON; AND THOU, MOON, IN THE VALLEY OF AJALON. And the sun stood still, and the moon stayed, until the people had avenged themselves upon their enemies. Joshua 10:12-13

Of course Joshua did not do this miracle in his own strength. It was God who kept the sun and moon in place. But He did it because His servant Joshua had spoken it in faith and simplicity. His servant had declared it, and so God was committed to performing it. This truth opens up to us all sorts of things that formerly seemed to be impossibilities. Our words can change the world in which we live. In fact, your life follows your words.

Words Alone

> *In most cases of praying for the sick, Jesus spoke less than ten words.*

With many of the sick Jesus healed, He didn't even touch them. Even when He raised Lazarus from the dead, He did it strictly with words.

In this case, it took only three words: *"Lazarus, come forth"* (John 11:43). That was all, but it was enough. With nothing more, Lazarus came out of the grave that had held him.

Jesus didn't have to go down into the grave, take Lazarus' grave clothes off of him, shake him, and say, "Lazarus, get up. Come on. Lazarus, did you hear me? Get up." He didn't have to address the demons of death, and He didn't have to recount the other details of the situation. He needed nothing more than those three words to get the job done.

In most cases of praying for the sick, Jesus spoke less than ten words. And those ten words or less never once spoke of the problem, only of the desired result.

What about your prayers? Do they reflect the truths found in our

The Necessary Example

Lord's prayers, or are they wordy? Do they address the problem, and not the desired result? Do you change your voice to sound more spiritual to convince yourself that you have faith that God can heal? Do you jump up and down, fall on the floor, or kick and scream to try to get God's attention? Do you try to interview the devil, asking what his name is, what he's doing at the moment, why, and how long he has been doing it? Such performances are not needed in order to get God to move on your behalf or to get the devil to flee. Just make your positive decree based on your knowledge of God's will in any given situation, and know that God hears and answers. Your lips then become the means of conveyance of God's deliverance from heaven to your point of need.

I prayed for a man at our church who had suffered a series of serious heart attacks, and God spoke to me and told me to go back and tell him something. I was to say, "You'll never die of a heart attack."

I did this, but as I was walking away again, the devil said, "What if he *does* die of a heart attack? What will you do then?"

I wasn't worried because that wasn't my problem. I had just repeated what God said, so I was sure that He would honor it. Even if He hadn't told me to say those words, He would have to make it good because I, His child, had spoken it in faith. If that man held on to his word from God, the devil could try to kill him in a thousand ways, but he would never die of a heart attack. I said he wouldn't, and God would honor our declaration of faith.

God did honor it. The man went to his doctor for an examination, and the doctor was shocked by what he found. Four heart attacks had left this patient's heart damaged and extremely weak, and doctors had planned to do surgery on him. Now, upon examining the heart again, the doctor found that it was completely healed. And more: it appeared as if the man had never suffered even the first heart attack—let alone four.

Needless to say, there was no need for an operation. The doctor sent him home saying, "I'll see you in six months!"

Not only was the man's heart healed, but he woke up the next morning to find that he was healed of the arthritis with which he had been suffering for years. And just like that man, this year you can walk in victory because you now realize that your lips get God's best from heaven to you. Your life follows your words. We have the example of Jesus, and we know that it will work for us too.

Just as Jesus' words were powerful, our words are powerful, and when we voice our desires to God in prayer (using the example of Jesus in the gospels), we get what we are desiring. Whatever you say in this way you will get. If you want to be a mighty man of God, stand up and declare it: "I am a mighty man of God. I am what God says I am. I am anointed. I have the anointing in my mouth, and whatever I speak I will have. I will not be defeated because I am the head and not the tail."

Speak what you want. Say it. Confess it in the simple terms, and then see it come to pass. Jesus did, and you can too.

Jesus Prayed His Desires

Several times now in the book we have looked at Jesus' words in Mark 11. Again in this present context, they are important:

> *And Jesus answering saith unto them, Have faith in God. For verily I say unto you, That whosoever shall say unto this mountain, Be thou removed, and be thou cast into the sea; and shall not doubt in his heart, but shall believe that those things which he saith shall come to pass; he shall have whatsoever he saith. Therefore I say unto you, WHAT THINGS SOEVER YE DESIRE, when ye pray, believe that ye receive them, and ye shall have them.* Mark 11:22-24

The Necessary Example

"WHAT THINGS SOEVER YE DESIRE, when ye pray, believe that ye receive them, and ye shall have them." As we saw in Chapter 2, this means simply pray your desires. This is exactly what Jesus did, and He showed us that if we can speak forth a thing that is on our heart without doubting, we can have it. If you only pray what you already have, that's what you will always get. So, it's time to reach higher, to pray beyond our current level.

When we pray our desires, we must be sure that they are also God's desires, His destiny, for our lives. Then we can be sure that He will bring them to pass.

As Jesus prayed His desire, never praying what He currently had, never praying the situation, only praying what He wanted to come out of the situation, that was exactly what He received. And you and I can do the same. This is a truth that we must all pursue further in the coming days.

Jesus Never Worried

Worry and fear should have no part in our prayers, just as they had no part in the ministry of Jesus. Paul taught the Philippian believers:

> **BE ANXIOUS FOR NOTHING**, *but in everything by prayer and supplication, with thanksgiving, make your request known unto God.*   Philippians 4:6

"Be anxious for nothing" simply means not to worry about anything. Worry, anxiety, and stress all work against our faith and bring us into bondage. The presence of these negatives hinders our miracle from coming to pass.

Can you imagine Jesus being worried or stressed out or otherwise upset about any circumstance of life? I can't. And since He is our example, we know what God expects of us.

We should note here that some have pointed to the words of Philippians 4:6 as if they gave us a license to recite a list of needs before the throne of God. That is not the case. This word *requests* means cravings or desires, not a list of needs.

That God is not asking about our needs is confirmed by the truth of these words found in Jesus' introduction to the Lord's prayer:

> *But when ye pray, use not vain repetitions, as the heathen do: for they think that they shall be heard for their much speaking. Be not ye therefore like unto them: for your Father knoweth WHAT THINGS YE HAVE NEED OF, before ye ask him.*
>
> Matthew 6:7-8

He's not asking about something He already knows about. He wants to know your deepest desires.

So we must learn to avoid wordiness and feigned eloquence in prayer. We must ask in faith and avoid doubts and fears. We must refuse to dwell on the problem or consider the circumstance, but rather concentrate instead on the desired outcome. When we pray in this way, we, too, will receive quick and unusual answers.

If you can learn to follow the example of Jesus' prayers, you are ready to pray the prayer of faith and see results as He did.

Chapter 12

B-E-L-I-E-V-E

For verily I say unto you, That whosoever shall say unto this mountain, Be thou removed, and be thou cast into the sea; and shall not doubt in his heart, but shall BELIEVE those things which he saith shall come to pass; he shall have whatsoever he saith.

Mark 11:23

Soon after I had preached the original series of messages on this subject in our church, I was scheduled to speak in a large conference where there would be thousands of women hungry for God. The night before, I was awakened at four in the morning.

As I lay there in the hotel bed, I was meditating on the Lord and pondering exactly what I should say in my allotted time. I had been preaching this message for over sixteen weeks now, and there was so much revelation inside of me. "How can I get these women to understand what it means to believe You in forty-five minutes?" I asked the Lord.

No sooner had I asked the question than I heard the Lord speak to me. "Tell them to say ..." He began, but then He paused.

I breathlessly waited to hear exactly what it was that I should tell these women to say, and it seemed like an eternity before the answer came.

When the Lord again repeated the first words, I wondered if He would ever tell me the rest. "Tell them to say, ..."

But then the answer I had been holding my breath for came, and it was powerful: "Tell them to say, 'Because Emmanuel lives, I expect victory every time.'"

I lay there in awe of what God had just revealed to me and repeated it over and over in my mind, "<u>Because Emmanuel lives, I expect victory every time.</u> Because Emmanuel lives, I expect victory every time. Because Emmanuel lives, I expect victory every time."

My God, I thought, *that's it. That describes exactly what it means to believe God in only seven words.* All that I had been preaching for the past sixteen weeks was summed up in those seven little words.

> *If God is with us, we can expect victory every time*

I began to praise God for what He had spoken to me, and as I did, the room seemed to illuminate with the word B- E- L- I- E- V- E. Out of each letter fell the corresponding word, and I saw: Because Emmanuel Lives I Expect Victory Every time."

I rejoiced and screamed for my assistant. "Shawna, get up!" I said excitedly. "Write this down! You won't believe what the Lord just showed me."

I had her write it down just as I had seen it, and when we looked at what God had said, we rejoiced together.

Because **E**mmanuel **L**ives **I E**xpect **V**ictory **E**very time

"God With Us"

I was so glad that the Lord had called Himself Emmanuel because it means *"God with us"*:

> *They shall call his name EMMANUEL, which being interpreted is, GOD WITH US.*   Matthew 1:23

If God is with us, we can expect victory every time, not just some of the time, but all of the time. So, whatever we are facing today, right now, we can expect victory.

Because God is with us, and He lives, I can face tomorrow. Because He lives, I can deal with any trouble that may come my way. Because He lives, I can overcome anything that Satan throws at me. Because Emmanuel is with me, I am never alone. That changes everything.

God promised that He would never leave me nor forsake me, and that He would be with me until the end:

Lo, I AM WITH YOU ALWAY, even unto the end of the world. Amen.　　　　　　　　　　　　　　　　Matthew 28:20

He hath said, I WILL NEVER LEAVE THEE, NOR FORSAKE THEE.　　　　　　　　　　　　　　　Hebrews 13:5

This is enough word to keep us until Jesus comes. This is all we need. Because He lives, we can expect victory every time. We may not know how the victory will come, but we know it *will* come because He lives.

This was the most powerful thing the Lord had ever spoken to me, and in the months since I received this revelation, I have often advised people to write the words somewhere in their Bible so they will never forget them. These simple words should be there to remind them that through every situation of life they are not alone. Emmanuel, God is with us, is with them, and because of that, they can be known as B-E-L-I-E-V-E-rs.

We Are Believers

Jesus called us believers (*he that believeth*, KJV), and so did Paul:

YOUR LIFE FOLLOWS YOUR WORDS

He that believeth [a believer] *and is baptized shall be saved; but he that believeth not* [an unbeliever] *shall be damned.*

Mark 16:16

And what concord hath Christ with Belial? or what part hath he that believeth [a believer] *with an infidel?*

2 Corinthians 6:15

Children of God everywhere are believers. They can count on the presence of Emmanuel in their lives, and because of that, they can have victory every time.

As modern-day Christians, do we really expect victory every time? Of course, we expect victory when we can see the end of a thing. But do we expect victory when no end is in sight? Do we expect victory when a doctor tells us there is no hope? Do we expect victory when our bank account stands at zero? Do we expect victory when a spouse walks out on us and says that they don't love us anymore? Do we expect victory when it seems that all hell is coming against our children? Do we expect victory when it seems that we are going down for the last time? Because God is with us, and none of our circumstances change Him, we *should* expect victory EVERY TIME.

It's rather a shame that we Christians have become fragmented and now call ourselves Baptists, Catholics, or Pentecostals. We should all want to be known more simply as believers. That's a fitting title for us, and we should be proud to bear it.

A believer is someone who is convinced, and if you are not convinced then your spiritual enemy can easily overcome you. If you are not convinced of the promise of God's Word, that *"greater is he that is in you, than he that is in the world"* (1 John 4:4), then the enemy can easily deal you a death blow.

We became believers through the process of exercising our measure of faith until it becomes a greater measure. We accepted the responsibility to believe, and now we must accept the other responsibilities that come with the title "believer." Now we must develop our faith so that we can believe for the impossible and lay hold of God's great promises.

A Believer Declares With His Mouth

Our faith is not just a mental assent. It is first thought, but then it must take the form of words. We first think right thoughts, and then we speak right words. In Mark 11, Jesus said the word *say* (*"say," "saith,"* and *"saith"*) three times and the word *believe* only once. We become true believers by speaking out the truth that has been revealed to us.

Jesus began this teaching by saying: *"Have faith in God"* (verse 22). He then went on to describe the law of faith and to show us how to have faith. Verse 23 is an important part of that teaching. Let us look at it once again:

> *For verily I say unto you, That whosoever shall SAY* [1] *unto this mountain, Be thou removed, and be thou cast into the sea; and shall not doubt in his heart, but shall believe that those things which he SAITH* [2] *shall come to pass; he shall have whatsoever he SAITH* [3].　　　Mark 11:23

There *is* the mental part to being a believer. We first believe with our mind, and our mind then engages our mouth to say the things we believe. Having been confessed, the belief then takes root in our heart. This is why it did not surprise me when the Lord said to me, "Just tell them to SAY, 'Because Emmanuel lives I expect victory every time.' "

Who were they to say this to? They could say it to themselves, to their spiritual enemy, or to anyone who tried to oppose them. It might be a parent, a spouse, or someone else who tried to make them doubt. Being a believer, they could say, "Because Emmanuel lives I expect victory every time."

It doesn't matter what you are going through, and it doesn't matter that it might look like you are in the worst shape ever, about as low as you have ever sunk. If you are a believer, that changes everything. You can expect victory every time—regardless.

A Believer Turns Truth Into Action

Believers turn truth into action. The interesting thing about truth is that it has no power until someone believes it. It cannot accomplish its work until it is believed.

The Bible, the Word of God, is powerful. It is sharp, *"sharper than any twoedged sword"*:

> **For the word of God is QUICK, and POWERFUL, and SHARPER THAN ANY TWOEDGED SWORD,** *piercing even to the dividing asunder of soul and spirit, and of the joints and marrow, and is a discerner of the thoughts and intents of the heart.* Hebrews 4:12

As powerful and sharp and life-changing as the Word of God is, it cannot work until someone believes it and stands upon it. Then it can do things beyond all human possibility or comprehension. But it would be possible to live in a warehouse full of Bibles and have no power because the Word is powerless, just a dead letter, until someone believes it and then speaks it out.

Men are constantly seeking answers for their problems, but they look everywhere except to God. Solomon said that men have *"sought out many [witty] inventions"* (Ecclesiastes 7:29). If that was true back in Solomon's day, how much more today. Modern men have devised clinics, rehabilitation programs, self-help groups, and many other types of programs to bring needed change to their lives, but sometimes none of them work. The Word of God, on the other hand, is *"quick,"* it is *"powerful,"* and it always produces the desired result. It is just waiting for someone to believe it.

With God's Word, you don't need twelve weeks or twelve steps. Sometimes just one simple word will do. B-E-L-I-E-V-E is just such a word: "Because Emmanuel lives I expect victory every time!" What else need be said?

> *With God's Word, you don't need twelve weeks or twelve steps.*

A Believer Never Quits

Believers never quit. When anyone backslides, it's because they no longer believe the Word of God. If they believed, they wouldn't quit. They would forge ahead, knowing that their reward is great.

When we are convinced that what we speak is the Word of God, that it was given for us, and that we need have no fear for its fulfillment, what can discourage us? Because Emmanuel lives, we expect victory every time.

A Believer Makes Every Promise Personal

The Bible was not written for someone else; it was written for YOU. Take the word that comes to you from it, and put YOUR name on it. When God speaks to YOU a personal word, a *rhema* word, take hold of it firmly and stand on it until it comes to pass.

Over the more than twenty plus years that I had been preaching the Gospel, I had preached a few times from Mark 11:23, but I had never made that verse my own. Now, I put my name on it. That was Darlene Bishop's verse. God was saying to me personally, "Darlene, when YOU speak to YOUR mountain and YOU tell it where to go, and YOU don't doubt in your heart, but YOU believe the thing that YOU say will come to pass, YOU will have whatever YOU say." That was now MINE.

A Believer Believes What He Preaches

Many preachers don't even believe what they are preaching, and sometimes it's obvious. You don't feel anything when you hear them speak. If they don't even believe it themselves, how can it possibly impact your life? If they don't believe it, why should I?

I would be willing to lay down my life for what I preach, and when people see that, they know my message is truth, and they are blessed. It happens because I am a believer. I not only believe everything I say, but I walk it out in my daily life. I never tell people to live one way, and then I live another.

A Believer Holds Fasts Until the Manifestation Is Seen

When I was suffering with a lump in my breast in 1986, several prominent evangelists prayed for me. Although I still did not receive the manifestation of my healing, I was fully convinced that I *was* healed. Believers pray, and then they hold fast to their confession until the manifestation comes.

Five more months went by, and still there was no manifestation of my healing, but I continued to believe God. Believers may get discouraged, but they never quit. They never cry out, "It looks like God doesn't love me," or "It looks like I won't make it." Believers are convinced. They know that Emmanuel is with them, so they have no fear.

Faith and fear cannot live in the same house. When fear comes in, faith has to leave. Real believers are free from fear, so they have victory every time.

Jacob Was a Believer

When his brother Esau was out to kill him, Jacob came to the end of himself. He sent his wife and children away and spent the night in prayer. There he wrestled with the angel of the Lord until daybreak.

Eventually, the angel asked him, "What is your name?" He wanted to see what was in Jacob, what his true character was. And what he found was not pretty. This man was Jacob, the supplanter, but God wanted to make him Israel, a prince with God.

"My name is Jacob," he confessed. "I've cheated everybody. I've been a swindler, a deceiver, a liar." When he admitted his sin, the angel changed his name and, with it, his character. And God can change you too. Emmanuel lives, He is with you, and he can give you a new name today.

Jacob's sin had caught up with him, and, at first, he didn't want to admit what was in his character. But when he began to dig down and pray through, he couldn't help but see what was really in him. Praying through brings honesty, and it can happen to you too.

Jacob was a believer because when he wrestled with the angel that night, he refused to let go until the blessing came. He said, *"I will not let thee go, except thou bless me"*:

> **And Jacob was left alone; and there wrestled a man with him until the breaking of the day. And when he saw that he prevailed not against him, he touched the hollow of his thigh; and**

171

the hollow of Jacob's thigh was out of joint, as he wrestled with him. And he said, Let me go, for the day breaketh. And he said, I will not let thee go, except thou bless me.

Genesis 32:24-26

That night, Jacob turned into another person because he held fast until the victory came, and you can do the same thing because Emmanuel lives.

Paul Was a Believer

Late in his life, the apostle Paul wrote to Timothy:

> *Believers never give up.*

I have fought a good fight, I have finished my course, I have kept the faith: henceforth there is laid up for me a crown of righteousness, which the Lord, the righteous judge, shall give me at that day: and not to me only, but unto all them also that love his appearing.   2 Timothy 4:7-8

Paul had *"kept the faith,"* even though it had not been easy. He had fought *"a good fight."* He had faced many obstacles and seen many tough times, but he could still say:

But none of these things move me, neither count I my life dear unto myself, so that I might finish my course with joy, and the ministry, which I have received of the Lord Jesus, to testify the gospel of the grace of God.   Acts 20:24

Paul was a believer. He knew Emmanuel, God with us, so he could expect victory every time. He must have thought, "It doesn't matter if I am in a jailhouse or at the bottom of a big pile of rocks. Even if I am snake bitten, or running for my life, I still expect victory every time."

Paul could say, *"None of these things move me,"* and he could say it because God had already shown him that He had made a way for his escape. Believers never give up. They hold on until the end because Emmanuel is with them, and they can expect victory every time.

My Mother Is a Believer

My mother prayed for forty years for the salvation of my brother Dale. He was the heathen of all heathens. I had never met anyone who was as bitter as Dale was.

Whenever I went to visit her, Mama would ask me to take her to Dale's house. He would see my car pull up and come out to greet me. But when he realized that Mama was with me in the car, he would say, "Get her out of here; I don't want to see her face."

Mama would cry at this and plead with him. "Please, Baby," she'd say, "I just want to kiss you. I just want to love on you a little. Please come over here and talk to me." But he always acted like the devil in her presence.

When we would leave Dale's house, I would say, "Mama, please don't make me do this anymore. Why do you always make me bring you over here?"

She'd say, "Because, Honey, I've been praying for him for forty years now, and one day he *will* be saved." Well, I can now report that Dale *is* saved. Believers don't quit praying and believing and confessing. They hold on until they see the thing for which they have had the promise all along.

Don't you quit praying and believing for your children, no matter how bad they get, no matter how many times they backslide, or how many times they are up and then back down. Don't give up. You can't give up because you are a believer. You know that your children are promised to you. You claimed them. You dedicated them to God. It doesn't matter what Satan says about them. If their salvation has to become a reality only when they are forty or even when they are sixty, God will bring them in because your faith is such that you expect victory every time. And it will be yours.

The Woman of Canaan Was a Believer

The woman of Canaan who asked Jesus to pray for her in Matthew 15:22-28 was a believer. She was not Jewish, so to the Jews, she was considered to be unclean. Still, she didn't give up hope that Jesus would heal her daughter—even when He called her a dog. Many of you would have lost faith about then. If a preacher ever told you, "Get out of here, you dog," you would lose hope.

This time, it wasn't a preacher who said it, but Jesus Himself. He told the woman that her people were dogs, and that it was not right for Him to give her blessings that belonged to God's children.

Her answer was interesting, "I may belong to a race of dogs, but I know that You have the words of life, and I want even a crumb of it" (my paraphrase). And she received her heart's desire that day. When you believe in God, you don't give up. Hold on until the very end, and you will be blessed.

There was no other place for this woman to go, and there may be some of you reading this book who have come to the end of yourself as well. You may well have exhausted every resource available to you in life, but God led you to read this book so that you would know that there is victory in your words. Your life follows your words. Hold them fast until victory comes.

A Believer Thinks Right

Your victory will come from what you say, but it always begins with your thoughts. David said:

> *Search me, O God, and KNOW MY HEART: try me, and KNOW MY THOUGHTS.*   Psalm 139:23

King Solomon declared:
> *As he [a man] THINKETH in his heart, so is he.*
>   Proverbs 23:7

Many times, when you see the word *heart* in the King James version of the Bible, you can replace it with the word *mind*. So, as a man thinks in his mind, so is he.

Jesus said:

> *Out of the abundance of THE HEART [mind] the mouth speaketh.*   Matthew 12:34

Thinking is the act of talking to your spirit, of talking within. You are your own best counselor—if your heart is filled with God's Word. Many times in life we think we require professional counseling, but if we would just reason within ourselves based on what God has said, we would usually come up with the right decision or the right answer.

What has God said about you and about your situation? Remind your flesh and your spirit of it.

You have to talk rough to your flesh because your flesh doesn't understand anything else. Tell your flesh, "You have to die because there is a spirit in me that ever lives to praise and worship God." That's right. Talk to yourself. Set your flesh straight.

The things that occupy your thoughts determine your relationship with God. What occupies your thoughts?

The Bible tells us to meditate on the Word of God day and night:

> *This book of the law shall not depart out of thy mouth; but thou shalt MEDITATE THEREIN DAY AND NIGHT, that thou mayest observe to do according to all that is written therein: for then thou shalt make thy way prosperous, and then thou shalt have good success.*
> Joshua 1:8

In Old Testament times, the children of Israel wrote God's words down and then hung it in various places on their garments. They made bracelets of it and placed it on their arms. They even draped it around their heads. They did all of this so they would never forget the promises God had made to them. Your spiritual enemy wants you to forget everything that God has said. He wants you to forget who you are, whose you are, and the power and authority you have.

You Are a Believer

But you are a believer, and you can know that because Emmanuel (God with us) lives, you can expect victory every time. Imagine that you are facing an impossible situation, and it seems that there is no way out. Then you look up and realize that God is with you, and because He is with you, He pushes you through a place you thought was impossible to pass. He walks you right through to the other side with ease. Now you don't worry about the situations you face because you know that because God is with you there is no problem you cannot conquer. You can do anything with His help.

You are a believer and can be victorious in all things because God is with you. He is not just beside you; He is *in* you. He said He would never leave you. He sticks closer than a brother:

B-E-L-I-E-V-E

There is a friend that sticketh CLOSER THAN A BROTHER.

Proverbs 18:24

A brother can't get *in* you, but God is *in* you, and when you stand up, God stands up in you. When you are going through something, God is in you saying, "Go on, you can make it. I am with you. I am in you. You can make it!"

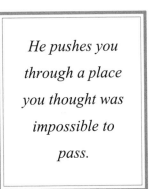

He pushes you through a place you thought was impossible to pass.

When I taught my children to ride a bicycle, I would hold them up until they got started peddling. They were afraid for me to turn them loose, but I would encourage them. "I've got you," I said. "I'm not going to turn you loose until you feel safe. I'm holding you up, and I'm not going to leave you. Just start peddling."

Sometimes they were still hesitant and I had to say, "Come on. You've got to do something. That's it. Just keep peddling now. I'm right here."

I would run along beside them for a while, until they felt more confident and could ride on their own.

This is exactly what God does for us. He is always right there with you, running alongside you saying, "Keep on peddling because you will go through. You can make it. Come on! Come on! You can make it. Because I am with you, expect victory every time!"

Take Something From It

If you receive just one thing I've written in this book, lay hold of the fact that you are a believer and because you are a believer, you are saved, healed, delivered, protected, preserved, and made whole.

YOUR LIFE FOLLOWS YOUR WORDS

If you can receive a second thing, let it be that because Emmanuel lives you expect victory every time.

Your expectation is what moves God because as your faith is so it will be unto you. Whatever you do, hold fast to your prayer of faith and just *say* "B-E-L-I-E-V-E."

Chapter 13

WAYNE'S RECOVERY

They shall recover.   Mark 16:18

I began this book by telling you about my brother Wayne and his phone call that stirred me to begin searching the Scriptures anew and to seeking God for the answers about why the prayers we Christians were praying for the sick were sometimes not working. I needed some quick answers.

The Challenge

The cancer had caught Wayne totally by surprise. He had gone to the doctor thinking that he was suffering from a lingering sore throat. When antibiotics didn't help, a biopsy was taken, and this led to the bad report he had called me with.

The doctors had given him one alternative to waiting for death to come. If he allowed them to take out his voice box and tongue, and he underwent the necessary chemotherapy and radiation treatments, he might live a while longer. But there was no guarantee. I knew that God wanted to heal him. He had said, *"They shall recover."*

"I would rather die than not be able to talk again," he told me on the phone. "So, I'm definitely not going to have the surgery."

I wasn't surprised by that decision. Wayne's voice was important to him. He had been a successful songwriter in Nashville, having written hits for such singers as Lori Morgan ("What Part of No Don't

YOUR LIFE FOLLOWS YOUR WORDS

You Understand"), Tim McGraw (a number one song, "Not a Moment Too Soon"), Holly Dunn ("There Goes My Heart Again") and others, including several for Toby Keith. More recently, he had been writing for the Backstreet Boys. His success as a songwriter was at its peak.

Wayne had been out of church for a while, and now he said to me on the phone, "Sis, I'm coming to your house, and I need someone to put some faith in me for what I'm going to have to face." Four and a half hours later, he was at the door. I had been praying about what I should do, and I felt that I had some answers for him.

The First Steps

When he greeted me, Wayne said, "Sis, can you believe that I have cancer?" He was obviously devastated, and tears were streaming down his face.

"Let that be the last time those words ever come out of your mouth," I told him. My studies on the power of the tongue had warned me that Wayne could curse himself with his words. Instead, I spoke positively to him: "I have just discovered in God's Word that when He saved you, He also healed you and set you free. You're already healed. We just need to stand on that word and believe God to see the manifestation of it."

When he had called, I had suggested to Wayne that he come and spend some time with me in my house so that we could have time to pray and believe God together. I prayed for him that night, and I began to confess his healing, then and every day thereafter.

As I learned new things each day about the need for confession, faith, right thinking, occasional rewinding, perseverance, passion, timing, and the use of Jesus' name and His example, I preached them in the church, and I put them to work on Wayne's case at home. It worked well that he had decided to accept my invitation to stay with us, and that I saw him several days of the week.

For a while, Wayne kept his home in Nashville and continued to drive back there to work on songs a couple of days a week. When he was with us, he plunged into the activities of the church, getting very serious with God, and so I was able to pump faith into him there. He sat and listened to that entire series of sermons I preached over the next sixteen weeks. And then we talked faith and rehearsed the promises of God together at home.

> *He plunged into the activities of the church, getting very serious with God.*

The Worsening of Symptoms

At first, the cancer was not visible on the outside at all, but within weeks after Wayne's arrival at our home, it had begun to spread from the inside to the outside, and large knots began to develop on both sides of his neck.

The internal part got worse too. Soon Wayne was having problems swallowing, and then he was having problems breathing. One night he was smothering so badly that we had to rush him to the emergency room. There, they inserted a trachea tube to help him breath. The tube became a permanent fixture. With these developments, he sold his home in Nashville, suspended his songwriting, and stayed with us at our home.

Wayne's sickness drug on through the spring, and by late summer he was a very sick man, unable to eat any solid foods and receiving his only nourishment through liquid supplements. His condition continued to deteriorate until, by September, he was down to eighty-four pounds. His doctor, upon examining him that September, told us that he would not be with us for the holidays.

When Thanksgiving Day arrived, Wayne sat at the table with the rest of the family, drinking his Ensure and watching the rest of us eat a hearty meal.

Every morning I continued to go into his room and speak positively to him about his future, but he was getting weaker.

"Sis, do you really think I'm healed?" he began to ask me.

"Yes, Baby, you're healed," I answered, "and don't you give up."

At times he had told me, "I'm so tired of fighting this; I don't know how much longer I can have strength to fight it."

"Don't give up," I encouraged him. "I'm not letting you give up. God has already healed you. Let's declare it together. God said that if we would decree it, He would establish it."

And together we would proclaim over him, "I am saved, I am healed, I am delivered, I am protected, I am preserved, and I am made whole in the name of Jesus."

The Christmas Crisis

By Christmas, Wayne was so weak that he could hardly walk and spent most of his time in a hospital bed. The knots on his neck kept growing and had now reached the size of baseballs. On Christmas Day, he said to me, "Sis, I'm starving to death."

And he was starving. His hair had begun to fall out—the result of malnutrition.

"Can't you drink some more Ensure?" I asked.

"It doesn't seem to be helping me," he said. "No matter how much of it I drink, I still feel hungry."

His son helped him out of bed and into the kitchen so he could be with the whole family, and there he spied a chocolate-covered cherry.

"Sis," he said, "do you think I could use my finger and just get a lick of that cream filling? It would taste so good. Anything at all would taste good!"

He hadn't been able to swallow anything remotely solid for so long that I was hesitant. But he seemed so pitiful and so hungry, and it was Christmas, after all. "Well," I said, "if you think you can handle it, go ahead and try."

Before long, Wayne was choking and strangling so terribly that it seemed that he would die right there before our very eyes. He turned blue, and we gathered around him to pray.

Eventually, Wayne recovered his breath and was returned to his room so that he could rest.

I continued to believe for and confess his healing. First thing each morning, I would go check on him. We had to have someone stay with him around the clock. If not, he would strangle during the night. Someone had to be there to suction the phlegm out of his throat. On New Year's morning, his son was with him, having stayed by his side throughout the night.

The New Year's Breakthrough

"How are you doing, Baby?" I asked Wayne that morning.

His answer amazed me. "You know, Sis," he said, "for some reason I feel like I could eat something."

"You do?" I queried, a little thrilled and a little cautious, remembering our ordeal with him at Christmas over his attempt to eat just one chocolate-covered cherry.

"I do," he assured me. "It's the funniest thing, but I feel like I can eat."

"Well, what would you like to have?" I asked, not wanting to discourage him in any way.

He grinned and said, "I'd like to have some of your cat-head biscuits with gravy, some bacon and eggs, and some fried potatoes."

"I'll have it ready and on the table in about thirty minutes," I answered, and I headed for the kitchen.

As I mixed up the biscuits that morning, I rejoiced: "Father, I thank You that Wayne is healed, and I thank You that he will be able to eat all of this." I kept confessing it.

> *In that moment, the earth seemed to stand still.*

Wayne's son helped him to the table, and together we prayed. We again thanked God for Wayne's improvement and agreed that he would be able to eat.

And then it was time for the test. Not one bit of solid food had entered his stomach in more than four months. The last time he had tried to take anything it had nearly killed him. What would happen now?

As that first bite moved toward his mouth, it seemed to do so in slow motion. All eyes were on Wayne as his hand moved ever closer to his opened mouth. Slowly the first bite went into his mouth, and he began to chew it deliberately. In that moment, the earth seemed to stand still.

Then, suddenly, Wayne's eyes lit up, and he turned to me. "Sis," he said with obvious joy, "you can't imagine how good this tastes," and he continued eating, rejoicing and praising God, groaning with delight, and oohing and aahing over the good taste of my cooking between every bite. He had not eaten any real food for so long that every bite was a sheer delight.

Before he got up from the table that day, Wayne had eaten two of those huge cat-head biscuits with gravy (for those who haven't heard of cat-head biscuits, they are named this because they are as large as the head of a cat), two eggs, fried potatoes, and I lost count of how many pieces of bacon—and he didn't even choke one time.

Recovery

And that was just the beginning. Over the next six weeks Wayne gained thirty-five pounds and with it his strength returned.

In March, he and his son took a trip to the Bahamas. In April, he went out and bought a new house in our neighborhood, closed on it and moved into it in May. His doctor gave him a clean bill of health, and told him, "Wayne, when you first came in here, I wouldn't have given you fifty cents for your future. If I ever saw a miracle, you are one.

That's how great our God is. Get ready to pray the prayer of faith over your loved ones, over your neighbors and coworkers, and over all those to whom the Lord will send you.

Chapter 14

PUTTING IT ALL TO WORK

All power is given unto me in heaven and in earth. Go ye there-
fore … .   Matthew 28:18-19

So the prayer of faith is a prayer of confession. It is a prayer of right thinking. It is a prayer cleansed of negativity. It is a prayer of perseverance. It is a NOW prayer. It is a prayer made in the authority of the name of Jesus, according to His example, and in His words. And it is a prayer that works because Emmanuel lives. If you have grasped these concepts, then you are ready to pray for the sick and see them recover.

Because of all that God has done in my own life, my burden these days is to raise up a generation of believers who can pray the prayer of faith and get results. I'm not talking about making everyone a preacher. Any simple believer who can pray the prayer of faith can cause hell to pull back.

Minister In Your Circle

But, since there are so many lost to be reached and so many sick to be healed, where do we begin? Start in your own circle of influence.

When Jesus was about to do the miracle of the loaves and the fishes, He told His disciples to sit the people down in groups of fifty. He then chose one disciple, gave him a piece of the bread and of the fish, and told him to use that to meet the need of the fifty to which he was assigned. When those fifty had eaten, he was to go to another group of fifty. In this way, every need was met among a great many people.

This is what God wants today in the Body of Christ as a whole, and this is what He wants for your life. His desire is that you give of your bread to those in your immediate circle. If you meet the needs of those in your circle, and your brothers and sisters in Christ do the same in their circle, the needs of many can be met. Imagine twelve men feeding thousands of people! Now, multiply that by the number of believers in the world today, and you will see that a great work can be done very quickly if enough of us pick up the mantle.

> *His desire is that you give of your bread to those in your immediate circle.*

This world is huge and the number of those who need bread from heaven seems mindboggling, but you have the bread, so give out to those you can reach, and trust God to use others where you cannot. He is faithful.

When you minister to those in your circle, you don't need a long prayer. All you need to say is, "Be made whole in the name of Jesus." You'll be amazed. It will work.

You will have more success if you seek out people who have needs similar to one that you had before you were delivered and made whole. Tell them, "Be free in the name of Jesus, just as I have been set free!" You have the bread they need, so you can now share it.

This is how God meant His ministry to go forth. If one well-known evangelist could heal the whole world, none of the rest of us would be needed. But every evangelist is just one man or just one woman, and many more hands are needed to accomplish the task before us.

When Jesus went away, He sent us the Comforter, and His power has been invested in the entire Body of Christ. We are all called to lay hands on the sick and to see them recover, to cast out demons and to see men and women set free. The promises of Mark 16:17-18, including casting out devils and laying hands on the sick to see them healed, are given to all *"them that believe."*

Personally I am looking to see the great I AM God working miracles through each member of the Body of Christ in the days ahead. I trust that this is your prayer, as a member of this great Body, and, if so, then so be it unto you.

Make Your Confession Today

If you are believing for God to use you in this way, call someone and make a public confession today. Tell them, "My life will never be the same from this day forward." I dare you to do it right now.

And, just as you have made this positive confession, your confession from this day forth, must consist of calling those things that are not as though they were. Don't say what *is,* for what is doesn't count. It has absolutely no weight with God. Think on those things that are eternal—on God's provision at Calvary through His Son for you—not on the things that are temporal (like your current standing).

Christianity has been called The Great Confession, and, as we have seen, our scriptures contain many great confessions that we can adopt as our own. Here are a few more examples:

> *God is able to make all grace abound toward you; that ye, always having all sufficiency in all things, may abound to every good work.*   2 Corinthians 9:8

YOUR LIFE FOLLOWS YOUR WORDS

Make it your own confession:

God is able to make all grace abound toward ME, that I, always having all sufficiency in all things, may abound to every good work.

When we confess this, we are saying that we possess all grace—abounding grace, saving grace, healing grace, baptizing grace, and all-sufficient grace. We are saying that we have all that we need to carry out God's will here in the earth.

Try another one:

With God all things are possible.   Matthew 19:26

Now, make it your own confession:

With God, all things are possible for ME.

When we confess this, we are saying, "I confess that all impossibilities in my life are possibilities with God." As children of God, we have the power to make bold statements like these, to confess impossibilities, and we cause them to come to pass.

This is what faith is—holding on when there seems to be nothing to hold on to, calling things that are not as though they were, declaring "I've got it" long before you can see it with your physical eyes. You must believe that no word that goes forth out of your mouth will return void, just as God said about the word that goes forth out of His own mouth:

So shall my word be that goeth forth out of my mouth: IT SHALL NOT RETURN UNTO ME VOID, but it shall accom-

plish that which I please, and it shall prosper **in the thing whereto I sent it.**

Isaiah 55:11

Once you have confessed something, then say, "I don't know when it's coming, but it's on it's way because I've already confessed it. It has already gone forth out of my mouth, and when the word goes forth out of my mouth, it will never return void. It has to produce the confession that I hold fast to. Once I have spoken it, it's too late for the devil to try to stop it." Now, take your rightful place and begin to minister to others.

Take Your Rightful Place

It is so wonderful to be saved, to know that we are God's own, and to know all of the great benefits He has reserved for us. With this, we can dance on the devil's head and let him know that his plans have been defeated.

You may need healing yourself. Just lay hands on the place you need healing, and say, "In the name of Jesus, this pain doesn't belong to a child of the King, and I will not accept it. I am healed." Now praise God for your healing. Your sickness will have to go, and then you'll be ready to minister to others.

So many of us have been held down by our current circumstances. It's time for us to break free and be able to free others.

God is taking His Church to a new level, and if the enemy is raging in your life, be encouraged. Anytime he comes in and tries to rattle you, it is because God is trying to take you somewhere you have never been before. Satan tried to rattle me with the bad news my brother Wayne received from his doctor, but he really messed up that time because it was that piece of bad news that caused me to seek God as never before and allowed me to discover new truths that brought me to this new level in God. And, since these are the truths I am now sharing with you in this book, in a sense the devil's mistake is allowing many in the Body of Christ to rise to a new level.

The year 2003 turned out to be a gloomy one for many people. Even as the year began, news commentators were reporting that we had never gone into a year with so much gloom looming on the horizon. One reporter in particular said that the events of the year would surely make the tragedy of 9/11 look like Sunday School. The whole world seemed to be expecting the very worst. The future looked dark, but when the world around us gets dark, we Christians can shine all the more. For the world, it was a gloomy year, but for the Church it was glorious.

We didn't need to concern ourselves with the countries claiming to have nuclear bombs. We were discovering a power that was above all other powers on the face of the earth. There was no bomb that could touch us, for God was *"for us,"* and the world had to get out of our way. As Paul wrote:

> *What shall we then say to these things? If God be for us, who can be against us?*   Romans 8:31

We knew what the Word of God said about us, and so nothing could discourage us or turn us aside.

At Solid Rock Church, Pastor Lawrence and I set about to produce people who were not only powerful enough to overcome their own problems, but could also help to pray others through to victory. We wanted more people who, instead of needing a prayer line themselves, could help to bring healing and deliverance to others.

Today, God is calling more of His children to become prayer warriors rather than those always "standing in the need of prayer." He has called us to lay our hands on the sick and to see them recover. Pastor Lawrence and I want to send out thousands of people who can do just that. We trust that other pastors around this country and around the world will do the same.

Reap the Benefits Through Heartfelt Confession

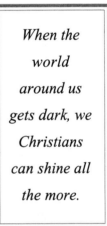

If you want to reap the benefits of this message, then keep it ever before your eyes. Place your decree somewhere where you will see it every day. Confess it, and decree, "I am a victor this year, because I am saved, healed, delivered, protected, preserved, and made whole in the name of Jesus!"

When the world around us gets dark, we Christians can shine all the more.

This is your year for miracles. I confess it, and I trust that you will too.

When you make your decree, say each line with heartfelt conviction and know what you are saying. Don't just repeat a bunch of words from memory because God doesn't honor empty words. Let the words come up out of your spirit. Stand up straight and tall. Take your decree in your hand, and say:

Lord, I thank You that I am saved because I called on Your name, believed in You, and confessed You with my mouth.

Lord, I know that I am healed because surely You bore ﹇q Truuia﹈ my ﹇our﹈ sicknesses and carried my diseases in Your own body, and by Your stripes I am healed.

I thank You, Lord, that I am delivered because You know how to deliver the godly.

I thank You that I am protected because Your angels are camping around me today because I trust You, and You deliver me.

I know that I am preserved, Lord, because You know how to guard Your children against every evil.

I am made whole today because you have promised not to withhold any good thing from me.

Hell had better look out because I know who I am in Christ Jesus, and I am aware of the benefits I am entitled to.

Get tough with the devil, and let him know that you know who you are. Proclaim your victory through declaration and then praise God for the manifestation of what has been declared. And you will see it come to pass.

Now Is the Time

If you are reading this book, and you are not saved from sin but you want what God has provided for you, pray this prayer:

Lord,
Forgive me for my sins. I want God on my side and all the benefits of His salvation. I believe His Son died for me, and I accept Him into my heart right now.

From now on, know that when you confess salvation, you are not just talking about salvation from sin, but also healing, deliverance, protection, preservation, and wholeness. From this day forth, be determined to draw closer to God each and every day.

Now, thank God for all of His benefits. You are saved in the name of Jesus. Praise God for the awesome truths that liberate and empower us for His work. Go and tell somebody about your decision today, and then, whatever you do, hold on to your confession in the days to come. Your life follows your words.

Now, you can begin praying the prayer of faith for those around you, and expect God to do what He has promised to do. He will save them and raise them up. Once you have learned to do your part, He will surely do His.

Reexamine Your Life

For those who are already saved, it might be in order for you to reexamine yourself. Paul wrote to the Corinthian believers telling them to examine themselves to see if they were still in the faith:

> *EXAMINE YOURSELVES, whether ye be in the faith; prove your own selves.*   2 Corinthians 13:5

That may sound radical, but when we are no longer loving like our Lord Jesus loved and caring for people as He did, can we truly say that we are still Christians, that we are still in the faith? Many of us are part of a great faith movement and of a generation of believers who claim to have what the disciples had at Pentecost. But why is it that more of us are not doing what the disciples did in the Acts of the Apostles? What's wrong with us? And why isn't our faith more effective?

It might be in order for you today to recommit your life to Christ and His principles, to tell Him that because He is Lord and Savior of your life, you will now do His will, not your own. With that recommitment, check your confession, your faith, your thinking, your perseverance, your passion, your sense of timing, your sense of remembering and of following Jesus' example, and then by all means, start reaching out to those around you. There is no doubt that the greatest joys in life come from serving others.

You are ready now to begin praying the prayer of faith and seeing the miracles you have long desired come to pass. Many of us have been taught that the day of miracles is over. But the manifestation of miracles has never been about a specific period; it is about a God who cannot and does not change. And it is He who calls you now to pray the prayer of faith, and to pray it with effectiveness.

God is calling you now to pray. Use the principles you have learned in this book to make it a prayer of faith. Declare it! Decree it! And receive your miracle!

Is any among you afflicted? let him pray. Is any merry? let him sing psalms. Is any sick among you? let him call for the elders of the church; and let them pray over him, anointing him with oil in the name of the Lord: and THE PRAYER OF FAITH SHALL SAVE THE SICK, and the Lord shall raise him up; and if he have committed sins, they shall be forgiven him. Confess your faults one to another, and pray one for another, that ye may be healed. THE EFFECTUAL FERVENT PRAYER OF A RIGHTEOUS MAN AVAILETH MUCH. Elias was a man subject to like passions as we are, and he prayed earnestly that it might not rain: and it rained not on the earth by the space of three years and six months. And he prayed again, and the heaven gave rain, and the earth brought forth her fruit.

James 5:13-18

MY DECREE

I decree that:

I am SAVED.

For whosoever shall call upon the name of the Lord shall be saved.
Romans 10:13

I am HEALED.

Surely he hath borne our griefs, and carried our sorrows:
... and with his stripes we are healed.
Isaiah 53:4-5

I am DELIVERED.

The Lord knoweth how to deliver the godly.
2 Peter 2:9

I am PROTECTED.

The angel of the Lord encampeth round about them that fear him,
and delivereth them.
Psalm 34:7

I am PRESERVED.

The Lord shall preserve thee from all evil.
Psalm 121:7

I am MADE WHOLE

They that seek the Lord shall not want any good thing.
Psalm 34:10

Who forgiveth all thine iniquities [SAVED];
Who healeth all thy diseases [HEALED];
Who redeemeth thy life from destruction [DELIVERED and PROTECTED];
Who crowneth thee with lovingkindness and tender mercies; who satisfieth thy mouth with
good things; so that thy youth is renewed like the eagle's [PRESERVED and MADE WHOLE].
Psalm 103:3-5